STORY WORKS

How Teachers Can Use Shared Stories in the New Curriculum

DAVID BOOTH

BOB BARTON

Pembroke Publishers Limited

For Myra Barrs, who has shared with us over the years her deep understanding of the role story plays in the lives of children.

© **2000 Pembroke Publishers**
538 Hood Road
Markham, Ontario, Canada L3R 3K9
www.pembrokepublishers.com

Distributed in the U.S. by Stenhouse Publishers
477 Congress Street
Portland, ME 04101
www.stenhouse.com

The publisher acknowledges the financial support of the Government of Canada through the Book Publishing Industry Development Program (BPIDP) for our publishing activities.

Acknowledgments

We wish to thank Larry Swartz for his classroom demonstrations of fine teaching, Ken Wood for his research and writing assistance, and the children and teachers of Lord Dufferin P.S. for their stories.

Portions of this book originally appeared in *Stories in the Classroom*.

Canadian Cataloguing in Publication Data

Booth, David
   Story works

Includes index.
ISBN 1-55138-125-7

1. Storytelling. 2. Language arts (Elementary). I. Barton, Robert, 1939- . II. Title.

LB1042.B63 2000   372.64   C00-931561-6

Editor: David Kilgour
Cover Design: John Zehethofer
Typesetting: JayTee Graphics

Printed and bound in Canada
9 8 7 6 5 4 3 2 1

Table of Contents

Introduction

Ten years ago, after each of us had spent thirty years teaching, we wrote a book called *Stories in the Classroom*. *Story Works*, a reworking and updating of that earlier book, is our story as teachers and colleagues over the last forty years.

Most school issues haven't changed in the last ten years, but some have. The basic principles of "storying" remain the same, but in some cases, the form and purpose have altered. Computers, for instance, can now enable young students to "publish" their own work in polished form, supporting their developing handwriting and artwork. Drama, once seen by some as a frivolous diversion, is now used to respond to difficult issues such as violence or prejudice in the schools.

We began teaching literature and drama in schools with classes on a rotary system, where one group after another would appear in our classrooms every forty minutes. Amid the scheduling nightmare, we found our hope and strength in story, stumbling as it were into "storying for a living." To involve our students and to save our lives, we began to explore all the ways and means of having the children work with stories — telling them, retelling them, reading them aloud, writing from them, dramatizing them, arguing about them, finding other stories like them — other versions, other authors.

The stories came in all shapes and sizes — anecdotes from home and playground, tales, legends, picture books, novels, poems, scripts, television shows, films, advertisements — and we grew more adept at using a story for all it was worth, both to save our strength and to help the children learn. We had not yet acquired much understanding of why story was so important for children, but it worked in our classrooms and so we continued. As we moved into working with teachers in in-service and pre-service courses, and with children in school settings, story retained its place at the centre of our work.

Now we have dozens of books by informed authorities on why story matters, why we should help children engage in storying. As well, we encourage children to tell and write stories from their lives, to polish them until they are personal touchstones; we now find stories of all kinds in bookstores for children and in libraries at home, in school, and in the community; storytellers are familiar sights at school celebrations.

This book attempts to address some of the challenges involved in making a storying culture come to life in the classroom. We found the most important factor to be classroom time with the whole class as a community of learners. With the new curriculum, the requirements of more formal assessment, the complexities of the social makeup of the children, alongside strong parental expectations, teachers are faced with crowded schedules and difficult decisions. We specifically set out to address these challenges in terms that would be of use to teachers who recognize the need for building a storying community. School life will function better and support individual needs if we can develop a classroom culture where we gather together to cooperate, collaborate and celebrate our common goals and achievements. We need to take time, as community members, to "meet in the town square", "around the dinner table", to share our concerns and our successes, to connect to each other, to recognize that we are all a part of a group who value and strengthen each member's contributions. We see our work in education as providing a framework for designing a storying time in the day (or during the week, or even the month), an occasion for participating together as a cohesive unit, anticipating and finding learning and satisfaction in shared experiences, where the others in our school life matter, and where we can grow independently because we are not alone. We may gather together on the rug for a story, come together to demonstrate our progress in a group project, engage in a class discussion on a common issue, join in reading aloud a series of poems from overhead transparencies, enjoy classroom books we have published, examine a particular strategy in a mini-lesson, or build a drama lesson from a story that puzzled us. What matters is that we gather together, and that our work focus on stories, those we listen to, those we read, those we tell, and those we create together.

David Booth
Bob Barton
Toronto
August 2000

"Oh Sarah," Ermingard whispered joyfully, "it is like a story!"
"It is a story," said Sarah. "Everything's a story — I am a story. Miss Minchen is a story."

Frances Hodgson Burnett,
The Little Princess

6

Why Story Matters

Me and my sister do our homework. Then we would watch TV. Sometimes we are nice to each other. Sometimes we don't like playing Barbie dolls. When we are done our homework, we look at the stars. We would say together, "In the sky, in the sky."

The stars look like they are a window so all the people who died in my family are looking down on us, like my sister Dannila, my great-grandmother and my grandfather and other people too.

When we eat grapes and we find a baby grape, we would say "This one is for Dannila," and throw it up in the sky. We would never see the grapes come down, so we think she grabs them and eats them up.

I love my sister Dannila. We believe in God and that is the end of my story.

Shaleta, Grade 2

We humans are storytelling animals. The drive to story is basic in all people, and exists in all cultures. Stories shape our lives and our culture — we cannot seem to live without them. As social participants in our world, we need real opportunities for conversation so that we can order our thoughts and make sense of our experiences. We pass the time of day in conversation, talk, chatter, exchanging ideas and stories.

I tell my story. You retell it, with all of your own life experiences playing upon it, and suddenly it is your story. Then we tell our two stories to a third member of the story tribe, who listens to both and builds a new, personalized version that shocks us with its twists and turns, and causes us to re-cognize our self. And we are present at the birth of a new story; we now have three for our story bag, and every time I choose one of those stories to share, I will unknowingly, unwittingly include bits and scraps from all of them and suddenly I am telling a different story, but it is still mine, and the story is inside, outside and all around my head. Such is membership in the story culture. We tell our own stories — our daydreams, our gossip, our family anecdotes. We become human through our stories.

Have we lost some of our sense of personal storytelling, or has the process altered? In a less technological time, people told each other their life stories regularly and productively, in times of friendship, trouble, celebration and mourning, engaging with each other, forging intimate alliances and creating their own identities. The need for a network in which we can safely story is still present, but we may have to search for others (even in virtual chat rooms) to listen to our tales, and to share their own experiences, to help us connect with "the other villagers in our lives" so that we can be a part of it all, so that we are included, so that we matter. It may be as simple as someone saying, "Guess what just happened to me," and someone else listening. We need to tell life stories to our loved ones, to share what we saw with our fellow workers, to gossip with friends, to talk to the people who sell us our groceries and our gasoline and fill them in on what has recently happened; we need to have a storytelling way of life. We give structure and order, through

Going back, way back, to the earliest of times, when men and women and children looked at one another, at the land, at the sky, at rivers and oceans, at mountains and deserts, at animals and plants, and wondered, as it is in our nature to do: what is all this that I see and hear and find unfolding before me? How shall I comprehend the life that is in me and around me? To do so, stories were constructed and told, and remembered, and handed down over time, over the generations.

Robert Coles,
The Call of Stories

telling stories, to our mountain of memories and emotions, making sense of and giving cohesion to our lives. And, of course, we tell ourselves stories 'in the head,' reweaving personal tales to ourselves from our own storylines of events that have captured us like fish in a net, worrying about what we will say next time, or replaying comments others have made about us, or remembering a holiday where life was so completely full. And sometimes these stories are told aloud with no one listening but the mirror in front of us or the empty chair beside us.

We need to consider the question asked by Jack Maguire in *The Power of Personal Storytelling*: "How do we break through all our compulsive, mechanical, awkward, ego-chatter to the stories that really matter, and to the tellings that are genuinely worthwhile?"

To become significant in a culture, a personal story needs to resonate with the listeners. Someone has to need our story to understand their own.

Constructing Our Stories

Stories are how we explain, how we teach, how we entertain ourselves, and how we often do all three at once. They are the juncture where facts and feelings meet. And for those reasons, they are central to civilization – in fact, civilization takes form in our minds as a series of narratives.

Robert Fulford,
The Triumph of Narrative

Sometimes a close friend, or even a therapist, will listen to our stories concerning painful experiences as we try to come to grips with or place a frame around what troubles us. This act of constructing a narrative can in itself help us perceive our situation differently by altering our particular point of view so that we may be able to see ourselves inside the tale we are weaving, and, in the most fortunate of happenings, even come to terms with the experience.

And how do we get better at telling our life stories, at recapturing the essence of what we think happened, at reflecting upon the experience, distancing ourselves until the universal connections peek through, so that we can share our stories with another, with thoughtfulness and delight, providing the listener with satisfaction from our tellings? And how true will our life stories remain as we rework them? We act as the artist/teller, shading what should be shadows, and illuminating what could be significant to our listeners.

As personal storytellers, we shape our memories through our mind's eye, adding intelligence and language power as we draw upon our spirit and soul. We need to find ourselves in our shaped retellings; we have listened to ourselves, imagining how others will hear our tale, how they will respond, modeling our telling on how others have shared their stories, attending to what works for the listeners each time we have an occasion to tell, consciously deepening and enriching the experience for everyone.

The human mind follows an imperative to narratize experience and to transform it, to share and compare with others. Harold Rosen says that the narrative that we construct "edits ruthlessly the raw tape."

Making Meaning as We Tell

Stories think, and they do it in the same way we do. This analogy to our thinking may explain why stories are so important to us and why they appear to be so meaningful. They speak to us, as dreams speak to us, in a language that is at once highly symbolic and childishly literal. They mirror our consciousness exactly because they are composed through a process both conscious and subconscious. We need to pay attention to the story, let its images pour through, and talk about them. And trust the story to do its work.

Through story, we can compare the worlds others create with our own representations, re-evaluate our feelings and ideas, come to terms with past experiences, enter into the lives of others, and hone our own abilities to predict and anticipate. Children play out their lives through story; it tells them that life will go on, and gives form to what has happened, what is happening, and what may happen, ordering their experiences through anecdote and tale. They need stories from us to give reassurance to their inner stories, the ones that demonstrate their curiosities, fears and concerns. And we can connect them to other people, other times, other selves, and, of course, other stories. In her book *Beloved*, Toni Morrison writes, "He wants to put his story next to hers."

Story is a continuous process. We borrow from others to see how our story fits theirs, then we remold it, add to it, alter it, tell it again anew, always exploring fresh possibilities.

Our second experience with a story is never the same as the first. We have changed and so have our expectations of the story. A Chinese proverb says that you can never step in the same river twice. When we as young children listen to stories, we develop the sense of narrative that will be the core of our thinking and languaging processes. The story continuum that will last for a lifetime begins in the earliest years, and continues forever. Children who are provided with a rich story environment — hearing stories, telling stories, reading stories, watching stories, and then talking about them — will grow as thinkers and as story-makers.

Narrative is not just a powerful way of validating one's life to oneself and to others; it can also be a useful tool for analysis and for assimilating one's understanding of scientific and technical concepts. How do we grasp such things as the big bang theory, evolution, the behaviour of the AIDS virus when it attacks cells, or anything we don't have the technical expertise to understand? Indeed, who has ever had, save perhaps Einstein, the technical capacity to comprehend such things? Quite simply, we describe it to ourselves as a story.

The writer Bell Hooks says that we have stories to support "the struggle of memory against forgetting." Stories do not offer simple meanings but form sets of meanings; listening to a story is a search for these meanings through the meanings we already possess. For this reason, encouraging the retelling of stories puts children in a classroom in touch with the many perspectives of others, and affords the opportunity to think deeply about implications as well as to realize that listening and reading are continuous transactions among "the tale, the teller and the told."

Story and Narrative

The research literature often talks about the two terms story and narrative, and it may be useful to note the differences: although all stories are narratives, not all narratives are stories. In *Stories Children Tell*, Susan Engel offers us a way of seeing these two terms: "A narrative is an account of experiences or events that are temporally sequenced and convey some meaning. A story is told with the intent to construct a full, cohesive entity for an audience, for someone to hear or read, even if the someone is the teller himself."

Children often embed bits and pieces of narratives in their conversations, or in their play, and these may become what Susan Engel calls "seeds of a future story." Young children, with receptive and encouraging adults, will gradually find delight in turning these seeds into full-blown stories, even telling the same story again and again, polishing the tale and strengthening their sense of story.

Connecting Story and Thinking

In popular belief, intelligence generally refers to one's ability to solve complex problems, while wisdom is seen as one's capacity to see the many sides of a problem and thereby draw reasonable analogies. Looking at this another way, Roger Schank says that intelligence is the ability to understand what has happened well enough to predict what might happen, and wisdom is the ability to tell the right story at the right time. In *Tell Me a Story*, Schank, one of the most innovative leaders in the field of artificial intelligence, looks closely at the way in which the stories we tell relate to our memory and our understanding. People talk about what happens to them, and they tell others what they remember. Telling stories and listening to other people's stories shape the memories we have of our experiences. Schank explores some of the remarkable aspects and implications of our ability to recall stories and relate them to new ones we are hearing.

Our interest in telling and hearing stories is strongly related to the nature of intelligence. We are even attempting to build machines that have interesting stories to tell and procedures that enable them to tell these stories at the right time. Our machines do not solve puzzles, nor do they do mathematics. Rather, our aim is to make them interesting to talk to, an aspect of intelligence often ignored by computer professionals and intelligence assessors.

Stories are generated from our memories of past events, and we use them to guide future actions accordingly. Memories allow us to coordinate past events with current ones to enable generalization and prediction. The calling to mind of prior experiences to help understand current situations often leads to new insights. Past experiences help make sense of new experiences, which is at the core of intelligent behaviour. Intelligence allows us to make sense of confusing prior events, as we draw on these events to interpret new events. As well, reasoning comes from experience, and differences in reasoning often depend on how prior experiences are coded in memory. Wisdom can thus be seen as experiences and stories, while intelligence is the creation and telling of story from experience.

When stories are retold, the words change, but the ideas remain more or less the same. The audience often determines the words chosen, and the ideas expressed may depend on the reinterpretation of past events in light of current events. As Schank states, "We may not even know what our own view of the world is until we are reminded of and tell stories that illustrate our opinion on some aspect of the world."

Story and Emotion

In *Fredrick*, Leo Lionni tells the story of Fredrick the mouse who was a storyteller. In preparation for winter, he spent his sunny summer days storing rays of sunlight, and gathering the colours and words of summer, while the other mice laboured day and night gathering corn, nuts and wheat. When the stored food runs out before the winter, the other mice are sustained by Fredrick's stories, nourished by the sun's warm rays, the colours of things alive and growing, and the desired words of warmer seasons.

Story can help us to gain an understanding of the complexity of our emotional responses, demonstrated by the expressive voices of characters speaking eloquently and powerfully of their feelings. We cannot teach children emotions; we can only help them reveal them and attempt to understand them. Children must filter their emotional experiences through their intellects, making sense of all kinds of information, turning story experiences over and over in their minds, integrating thought and feeling. Aidan Chambers says that children can think and feel with the images that story offers them, storing them in the "museums of their minds" and classifying them for later use.

Stories do things to people. We know that things happen to people when they read or hear stories, that any theory about the place of story in schools has to begin with this fact. Story is not an exercise in explanation or persuasion, but an experience between the teller and the told.

Story can cause us to tap into the universal situations of life, to stand in the shoes of others in all the world's past, present and future, taking risks, suffering, sorrowing, laughing, wondering, challenging, feeling satisfied but, most of all, tuning into the archetypes of all story wisdom.

How a storyteller feels about an event can determine how (or if) it is remembered. The emotional intensity of an experience will influence the way the memory is in the storytelling. In considering a story truth, we need to attempt to understand what we think the teller might have been feeling, thinking and doing at the time of the experience, as well as the effect of the context of the telling — who is listening and why, and what the consequences of the telling will be.

Story and Therapy

Understanding human behaviour through storytelling is a strategy used in several different areas of psychology. In *The Multicolored Mirror*, George Howard sees the development of identity as an issue of life-story construction: psychopathology as instances of life stories gone awry; and psychotherapy as exercises in story repair.

Therapy often begins with an invitation to the client to tell his or her stories: "Can you tell me what brings you here?" or "How can I be of help to you?" or "What seems to be the problem?" Clients understand that they are to tell the part of their life story that appears most relevant to their life problems.

This is my world – the world I understand and operate within best.

Through telling the story of his or her problem, the client provides the therapist with a rough idea of his or her orientation toward life, his or her plans, goals, ambitions, and some idea of the events and pressures surrounding the particular presenting problem. Over time, the therapist must decide whether this problem represents a minor deviation from an otherwise healthy life story. Is this a normal, developmentally appropriate adjustment issue? Or does the therapist detect signs of more thorough-going problems in the client's life story? Will therapy play a minor, supportive role to an individual experiencing a low point in his or her life course? If so, the orientation and major themes of the life will be largely unchanged in the therapy experience. But if the trajectory of the life story is problematic in some fundamental way, then more serious, long-term story repair (or rebiographing) might be indicated. So, from this perspective, part of the work between client and therapist can be seen as life-story elaboration, adjustment or repair.

Therapy might be seen as a cross-cultural experience wherein two life stories come together and each life trajectory is altered by the meeting.

We are in the process of creating value in our lives — of finding the meaning of our lives. A life becomes meaningful when you see yourself as an actor within the context of a story — be it a cultural tale, a religious narrative, a family saga, the march of science, a political movement, and so forth. Early in life we are free to choose what life story we will inhabit — and later we find we are lived by that story. The eternal conflict of freedom versus destiny is revealed in the old Spanish proverb: Habits at first are silken threads — then they become cables. The same could be said of stories. Thus, a paraphrase of one of Shakespeare's more dire warnings becomes appropriate: Beware of the stories you tell yourself — for you will surely be lived by them.

Teachers aren't therapists, and classrooms aren't clinics, but often telling our personal life tales can be therapeutic, and we recommend building occasions with young people for shared storying events at which we listen to the narratives from each other's lives, and learn about ourselves in the tellings.

Building Community through Story

Bob Barton writes:

Television is often singled out as the scapegoat for diminished storytelling in families, communities and organizations, but in her excellent book *Keeping Family Stories Alive*, author Vera Rosenbluth comments on the changing pattern of families and how this has contributed to the demise of so many family stories. "Families that once lived for three or four generations in the same geographical place and absorbed the stories which were handed on have now been spread out across the face of the globe," explains Rosenbluth. "The stability families enjoyed in the past has now been replaced by mobility and with that mobility much contact between generations and family members has been disrupted." Rosenbluth cites other factors too such as the high rate of marriage breakdown and in general the accelerated pace of modern living.

Story is a social process; we transform it as we tell it to fit the way we think. Our telling is shaped by everything in our life and our culture. We gain membership in our cultural community by telling stories.

The Anatomy of Story

Consider the language children meet in a story: words they can absorb into their own language data bases; expressions that range from the archaic to the jazziest contemporary slang; patterns that ring in their ears and seduce them into joining in. How much fun it can be to share a good story, to be delighted or surprised by words artfully arranged to create a narrative. Children tune in to the wonders of language, to the power that lies in becoming the one who stories.

Given the opportunity, children come to know the anatomy of story: its forms, genres, motifs, patterns, universals, words and images. Story acquaints children (even those who do not or cannot read) with a variety of language patterns, some of which may be outside their language community. It can familiarize them with literary language, an awareness they will need as readers and writers. And the words that are found in story — Where else would a child meet them? Words from other times and places, words found only in print, shared by storytellers with magic literary storehouses, idioms, expressions, metaphors, allusions — all to be met and savoured, some to be retained in the mind's eye.

. . . the goal of every storyteller consists of fostering in the child, at whatever cost, compassion and humanness, this miraculous ability of man to be disturbed by another being's misfortune, to feel joy about another being's happiness, to experience another's fate as your own.

Kornei Chukovsky,
From Two to Five

13

Children will meet familiar words used in interesting and unusual contexts, words that tumble and scramble and fall, engorged with meanings. We know that, as teachers, we need story words for our children, to take them further than we could alone, to touch them more deeply, and to delight and chill them with language far outside the confines of the classroom.

What a place to begin — a story. You can enter it at will, look around, run for cover or stay and consider the events in relation to your own world, reconcile the contradictions, contemplate the ideas, the emotions, the events, the relationships.

Why Children Need to Story

Young children need to story. They can find "self" inside the act of storying, as they try to order and communicate their thoughts, constructing both the story and their identity in the process. In *The Meaning Makers*, Gordon Wells found that

> ...as they narrate those experiences to others they are, perhaps for the first time, discovering their significance for themselves. These are the conditions that foster language development: when one has something important to say, and other people are interested in hearing it. It is then that language and thinking most fully interpenetrate in the struggle to make meanings that capture what one has observed and understood and communicate that understanding to others.

When we as teachers and parents examine the content and the construction of the stories children tell, we can gain insight about the ways in which children of different ages and stages use story in order to construct how they think and feel about their world.

We now have a documented body of knowledge by researchers who have carefully observed, recorded and studied language learning in childhood. The British researcher Michael Halliday, in *Learning How to Mean*, described what his son Nigel said and heard during his first years. These data formed the basis of Halliday's theory of language acquisition. Understanding what children use language for — what Halliday labeled as the functions of language — can show us what aspects of language use develop over time. In *Cushla and Her Books*, Dorothy Butler described her severely handicapped granddaughter Cushla's interactions with the children's books they shared together, and documented Cushla's amazing progress. Glenda Bissex recounted the story of her young son's beginning attempts at reading and writing in her moving book *Genyios at Work*. In *Prelude to Literacy*, the Cragos studied their daughter's interactions with reading between the ages of three and five. In her book *At the Very Edge of the Forest*, Carol Fox discussed the imaginative storytelling of five preschool children who had had extensive experiences with stories being read aloud. The author's analyses of these rich and complex children's stories add to our understanding of the linguistic and cognitive growth in story power. In *The Braid of Literature*, Shelby Anne Wolf and Shirley Brice Heath document the development of Wolf's two daughters who were learning to explore the intertextuality of their lives, blending real-life experiences with the make-believe world of story. Jerome Bruner said about the book: "It is for those who care about the miracle of literature that life imitates."

Bob Barton's granddaughter Emily, when she was almost three years old, retold the story of "The Three Little Pigs" as her nursery school teacher scribed it. Then Emily added her drawings.

Evidence presented in volumes of research over the past few years confirms that children who come from homes where storying is a daily activity and where stories and talk are plentiful anticipate learning to read with pleasure and indeed often turn up at school already able to do so, while children who have not had this experience are often the ones who find learning to read difficult. How can we as wise adults responsible for children nourish and strengthen that developing narrative framework, especially when it has such impact upon developing literacy? In *The Meaning Makers*, Gordon Wells's account of a fifteen-year study of English children's literacy and language growth, he states that "It was the sharing of stories that we found to be most important." In fact, telling and listening to stories appears to make as significant a contribution to early literacy as reading print.

In such instances, sharing stories with children is crucial in order to take up the slack, but it's also essential to continue the practice with those for whom it is already established. Reading, telling stories and poems, and sharing picture books are major planks in early reading programs at school. Such activities must continue to enrich the language arts program throughout the elementary and secondary years.

Story and School Violence

There is much concern today about increasingly aggressive and anti-social behaviour displayed by some children at school, at home and in public places. Growing numbers of teachers report having to spend more and more time dealing with outbursts of anger, disruptive behaviour, interpersonal conflicts, negative attitudes and defiance of authority both in and around school.

The school shootings of the past few years have horrified and outraged people everywhere, raising many fears from a decline in public standards to a lack of respect for a nation's institutions (schools, social service agencies, judiciary, the church).

In North America, many have questioned the role of television, which is the primary source of entertainment and values for most children. Do media representations of violence shape children's notions of how the world functions? Do these images and others like them affect how children and those they come in contact with should relate? What should be done to counteract this force?

In addition to the effects of media, child care professionals tell us that more and more children are experiencing conflict at home, that there is increased substance abuse within the family and that many of today's children have less access to the significant adults in their lives.

In an attempt to deal with these issues, many school districts throughout North America have implemented programs to help children manage behaviour acceptably and to have some control over the powerful feelings of rage and aggression that are in all of us. Halting bullying and controlling unruly behaviour can be done by policing, but if education is to do its job it must enable students to internalize appropriate behaviour which will continue where they aren't supervised.

Key skills which are addressed in these programs include problem solving, anger management, assertiveness and impulse control. By means of modeling, practice and reinforcement, the programs aim to develop in children the ability to recognize, experience and respond to the feelings of others and to learn to help themselves.

We urge that the words of Ted Hughes — "Story is the only language understood by the whole mind" — be heeded and that story be seen as a powerful force for helping students to make connections and for giving them scope for thinking in new ways.

Writer Arlene Moscovitch, in a paper on media violence, says:

> There is almost universal agreement by those dealing with incidents of violence against women and children that the actual underlying issues have to do with power and control. All children no matter how loving the homes in which they have been raised know about power... they are subject to it daily. Having first-hand experience of the use and misuse of power, however, is different from being able to name it and explore it in order to discover different ways it might be exercised.

Bob Barton writes:

Recently I worked with a class of fifth grade students on "Mart Was My Best Friend," a poem by Michael Rosen, a first-person account of betrayal by a friend. Two boys are standing at a bus stop after school. Suddenly one of the boys snatches the other's woolen hat from his head and tosses it over a wall.

> . . . I loved that hat
> It was warm and tight.
> My mum had knitted it
> and I wore it everywhere.

The aggressor taunts his victim:

> ... "Aren't you going to get your hat?"
> he says. "Your hat's gone," he says,
> "Your hat's over the wall."
> I looked the other way.

As the bus draws near the tension mounts. The boy who has lost his hat is fighting to gain control of a bad situation but all he can think about is what his mother is going to say.

> "Why didn't you go for it?"
> and what am I going to say then.

The bus arrives, the boy gets on without his hat. His adversary, incredulous, boards behind him, exclaiming,

> "You've lost your hat"
> "You've lost your hat"

At home, the boy tries to explain the missing hat to his mother. "You make me tired, you do," is all the comfort his mom can muster.

I asked the students to select a "worst moment" from the poem and read it to another classmate. Once they had swapped bits they were to discuss with each other the reason for their choice.

We reconvened as a large group to share our ideas. The majority of the students chose this moment:

> I was really scared I'd never get it back
> But I never let on
> I never showed it on my face
> I just waited.

In discussing why this was an awful moment, one boy summed up what many were feeling but couldn't express. He said, "I would feel so helpless that my friend was being mean to me that I wouldn't be able to do anything."

In response to his observation many of the children related personal experiences of a similar nature and talked about their feelings. A few hardier types knew exactly how they'd handle the situation:

> "I'd smash Marty in the face with a brick."
> "I'd run and tell the principal."

"I'd get my older sister to beat him up."

"I'd hire a lawyer and make him pay for damages."

But so many more felt the sadness of having a friend turn against them. They had no idea what to do. They needed time to think. And there was one boy who remarked, "I can't believe his mother's words!"

In the poem, by the way, the hat is returned that evening by Marty with no apology given. We are left at the end to wonder what will happen when the two boys stand at the bus stop the following morning.

Telling and Being Told

Anne Fine said in a speech in Toronto: "When you live through a bad situation you are often numbed by it. When you read about it happening to someone else then you come to understand from the safety of a spectator."

Our experience tells us that even the less threatening look at difficult issues from the spectator role will require time and patience. Memories will need to be shared.

Stories train and educate our sensibilities and our emotional responses. Through their strong appeal to the imagination they offer pathways through the difficult stuff of our existence. They are wonderful windows of opportunity for parents and teachers to develop stronger and more flexible skills for settling conflicts, bolstering self-esteem and emphasizing the need for gender equality. Development in these areas is crucial to helping minimize the possibility of young people resorting to violence in interpersonal conflicts. During the past three decades, contemporary writers have provided a steady stream of picture books, illustrated stories and novels aiming to help children understand the world they are growing up into.

At their best these books serve as moral templates and shed light safely and sideways for their young readers. At their worst, we get problems with stories grafted on to them, books that burden children with anxiety, and books that present the world as a dangerous and scary place. These types of books have no place in our work. We are not saying that all stories should end happily, but they need to offer hope to young people and encourage them to overcome difficulties and stand up to wrongdoing. In the story, the dog may die but there must be a puppy.

Children today need to learn tolerance, understanding, and getting on with others, and among the best examples of stories which emphasize these qualities are the world's folktales. These "stories of the tribe" provide strong reading and listening materials for children. The context of "long ago" enables children to explore a variety of problems and concerns that have troubled humanity forever, but in a safe, non-threatening framework. The deeds of heroes, the schemes of tricksters, the lore of nations past, can all serve as settings for children's own development — family situations, societal difficulties, supernatural beliefs and natural phenomena.

In many book experiences in school, children study a story, answer questions about it and explain what they like or dislike about it; but seldom do they engage in narrative, in practicing the art of storying, in developing their story sense. We would propose that using narrative as a means of expression and reflection, a way of sharing memories, should be the core of the curriculum. We learn to story by storying.

Many children in that fifth grade class we spoke of earlier had difficulty expressing their thoughts and feelings when it came to talking about Rosen's poem. But they had ideas. They needed time for conversation so that they could order their thoughts. They needed time to bring to the poem memories of their own experiences. Through storying they were learning to become reflective participants and spectators.

Encouraging Narrative Development

What can we as parents, teachers and other adults do to encourage the development of both a love for and an ability to tell stories, participating in the world of narrative that lets us share our lives with others? Here are Susan Engel's six suggestions:

- Listen attentively; the listener can help in the shaping of the story.
- Respond substantively as a true listener, rather than just as a critic.
- Collaborate by asking questions that help shape and direct the child's story.
- Provide a multiplicity of voices and genres, choosing stories and poems because they are told in interesting ways, or because they have beautiful language.
- Encourage the use of a wide range of story forms as children try to express and create themselves through their stories.
- Permit stories about things that matter, for the impulse to retell is powerful.

These all contribute to the development of the self and to the development of the second world — the one that allows us to live in the past, the future, the impossible, the world of narrative that allows us to share ourselves with others.

Stories Frozen in Print

Access to books is vital to a teacher's success with story. Bookstores that specialize in children's books, libraries within the school and community, conferences where new books are displayed, guest authors and storytellers, books about books written for teachers and parents, books on video and film, tape and CD, books that we loved as children, books that surprise and shock us into reading, book lists from computer

NAPOLEON

Children, when was Napoleon Bonaparte born, asks teacher.

A thousand years ago, the children say. A hundred years ago, the children say. Last year, the children say. No one knows.

Children, what did Napoleon Bonaparte do, asks teacher.

Won a war, the children say. Lost a war, the children say. No one knows.

Our butcher had a dog called Napoleon, says Frantisek.

The butcher used to beat him and the dog died of hunger a year ago.

And all the children are now sorry for Napoleon.

Miroslav Holub,
Gangsters, Ghosts and Dragonflies

sites . . . all these possibilities must be followed if a classroom is to be story-rich, not story-poor.

David Booth writes:

A teacher came into my office and gasped at the books on the shelves, on the floor, on the desk. She said that she had found a fairyland for children and teachers. When asked about books in her classroom, she replied that she taught special education and that there was no money in her specialty for such things. And yet her students may be the children who have most need of story entertainment — children who are afraid of print or who are preliterate, or with another language as their native tongue, children for whom printed story has not been a natural acquisition. The lure of skill sheets for unskilled readers is strong, but what we need are language experiences that open up story and release print power. Children who have not as yet been awakened to literacy must be drawn to it, so that they feel that they want it and need it. They require all kinds of experiences with books: at home; in the classroom; in school and in public libraries; and in book clubs and bookstores. They must develop an ease with story and with all print, so that difficulties do not deter them from the meaning making for which they are searching. They must become people who see print as always possible, and who feel comfortable with narrative patterns that lead them to associate story with learning and satisfaction. School and story can be partners in developing the potential of children. If stories do not touch a child in some way, then their strength will not become part of that child's life. Lifeless stories, stories written to convey messages, stories with stereotyped situations or people, stories too far away from the child's connections — these stories seldom affect a child. Good stories enrich and extend all types of knowledge, and become patterns and ideas for future learning and literacy. All children need books; those without them or those for whom books are unfriendly objects need them more.

How Stories Shape Our Lives

The sharing of stories with children has been a life mission for author Bill Martin, Jr. For him, stories are the most effective means of establishing that "great lifeline known as rapport." If we wish to interest children in education we must make it interesting, and not only do stories help to develop positive attitudes towards teachers and towards school, they also provide a rich source of ideas around which minds can come together. If we want children to make words work for them, then we must surely be prepared to demonstrate that words can work in pleasurable ways.

Stories offer us good counsel and can be a source of comfort, connecting us to other aspects of life: they put us in touch with larger things like laughter, love, mercy and compassion. Stories can cause us to raise profound questions and shape the landscape of our minds for the whole of our lives.

The children interviewed by Donald Fry for his book *Children Talk about Books* indicate in their comments that, for them, stories provide a "living through" experience, not just a "knowing about." It is from the stories that deeply involve them that they see played out the facts of their own lives that concern them deeply. "We learn from experience in fiction. Stories are not just amusements."

Literary story is missing in the lives of many children. Aside from television's passive, non-interactive storying, some children hear no stories read or told until they go to school. With broken families, crowded schedules, new curricula, and urban development comes the tragedy of children without a storehouse of stories. Grandparents who might have told stories may be unavailable or live far away; the home may not be a storying place; books may be foreign objects; television may dominate the home and limit talk-time; parents may be shift workers; single parents may lack time and energy for sharing story; crowded homes may lack quiet places for reading silently; storytelling may not be considered a significant experience by the adults in the home. It may be that school will have to bear the burden of story on its shoulders, that teachers will be the storytellers who reach most children. And yet with the burden come the related strengths that accompany story in school: curriculum connections; embedded literacy situations; tribal circles of shared experience; modeling of story strength by adults; a sensitivity to authors and illustrators, along with a recognition that the child belongs in this authoring relationship; a wide range of story content, chosen to broaden the child's experiential background, and inclusion of a body of story that carefully and subtly looks at issues of identity, community, sex, race, equity, culture and so on, and constitutes an exploration of genres and modes of story that may be unavailable to a child at home; books by a diversity of authors — North American, South American, Australian, New Zealand, European, African and Asian, male and female, old and young, books out of print, books hot off the press.

We need to cause that story to become bigger and better by showing it in slow motion, to make it possible for young people to get the best vision and the strongest memories of stories that they can. We can help them give life to the possibilities each story holds.

My mother read to me from the time I was a baby, and once, when I was three or four and she was reading my favorite story, the words on the page, her spoken words, and the scenes in my head fell together in a blinding flash. I could read!

The story was "Little Red Riding Hood," and it was so much a part of me that I actually became Little Red Riding Hood. My mother sewed me a red satin cape with a hood that I wore almost every day, and on those days, she would make me a "basket of goodies" to take to my grandmother's house. (My only grandmother lived in Rhode Island, three hundred miles away, but that didn't matter.) I'd take the basket and carefully negotiate the backyard, "going to grandmother's house." My dog, Tippy, was the wolf. Whenever we met, which in a small backyard had to be fairly often, there was an intense confrontation.

Trina Shart Hyman,
Once Upon a Time

Which Stories Touch Our Lives?

- Stories our friends tell us, sometimes in confidence
- Stories that are happening as we tell them
- Stories that we used to tell
- Stories that we overheard
- Stories that appear in our dreams
- Stories that we borrow
- Stories that we embroider

- Stories from other times
- Stories from other cultures
- Stories that confront stereotypes
- Stories in other languages
- Stories that pass on traditions
- Stories that remain unfinished
- Stories that teach
- Stories that persuade
- Stories that strengthen
- Stories that comfort
- Stories that frighten
- Stories that are sometimes forbidden
- Stories that explain
- Stories that amuse
- Stories that are spiritual
- Stories that make us remember
- Stories that help us to forget
- Stories that foretell our futures
- Stories that make us human
- Stories that define and redefine our experiences
- Stories we don't as yet understand
- Stories that are important to others

Life Stories

My Father: The Freezer Repairman

It was a hot and sunny day and the freezer was not working. My father was anxious to fix it so we could freeze some ice to cool ourselves off. My mom was watching him and telling him not to take out the screw that was sticking out.

My dad said, "I know what I'm doing!"

Suddenly the screw popped out and it hit him on the head. My mom and my brother Peter and sister Tammy were laughing at him. At first my dad was mad, but soon he started laughing too.

And that was the end of his job as Freezer Repairman.

Bryce, Grade 5

It is the business of schools not only to pass on the stories of the past but also to encourage the children to tell the stories of their own lives, the stories of their own making. For many of the students this respect and understanding of story's central place in our lives may never have been fully valued.

Children are in a privileged position as they develop into storytellers and storymakers, not fitting easily into stages or ages, but working with stories in order to understand the process of building life narratives, telling their tales out loud to find out what they have said and how they could say it more effectively. In teaching storying power, we must remember Eve Merriam's wise advice: "It takes a lot of slow to grow." But do we stifle their story impulses in school with unnatural silence, even sometimes removing recess from a crowded curriculum? When and to whom will they tell their tales, honing them, tuning in to those who are listening, learning what works in storytelling, learning what compels the listener to listen? And when will their crafted life stories connect with literature, where they can borrow the shapes and cadences, the words and phrases, of the professional authors they have loved in print, or that they have heard read aloud by generous parents and teachers? It is then that the young tellers will enter the world as storymakers, understanding more of the world though story.

As storying teachers, we can find ways to both inspire and enable our children:

- to call upon their memories of life experiences as starting points for building stories;
- to turn their stories into tales worth telling to others;
- to make the stories of others into their own, not through memorization, but through reworking, retelling and reliving them until they are deeply embedded in their story chests;
- to be guided and inspired by other memorable story experiences told by significant tellers who matter;
- to seek opportunities for listening to and telling carefully crafted personal life tales in natural and authentic ways that serve well the teller and the told, investing each story with meaning and art;
- to gain insight into their own stories through the process of sharing in the story circle, deepening their own storytelling practice and transforming themselves from within the tales they tell of their lives thus far;
- to be strengthened by the storying process so that competence, confidence and self-esteem will accrue and be part of other public speaking activities.

Nurturing Life Stories

We need to know more about how inner-city young people tell and receive stories and find meaning from these life tales in their everyday lives. The ethnographer and writer Shirley Brice Heath offers us a framework for creating story searchers out of our students:

- Learners can work in small groups to record, transcribe and study stories collected from family members and friends. They use these stories in class to develop questions to ask storytellers and listeners about the functions and evaluations of stories and to compare the kinds of background knowledge expected for each story to be comprehensible.
- Following such small-group work, the class creates a composite picture of the regions, cultures and languages reflected in the stories of the class. Some whole-class discussion enables students to prepare for more small-group work in which they consider themes, structural features and uses of particular techniques of style in the stories they have collected.
- Further small-group work centres on talking about differences and similarities of themes, uses of particular structural characteristics (such as setting and character descriptions, dialogue and references to folklore, myths and proverbs), and occasions and purposes of telling stories. Each group works out a comparative chart

of such features, identifying stories also by their region, language and culture of origin.

- Beyond and within these group exchanges about stories, learners can write their own stories to contradict, expand or parallel those they have collected. For example, elders being interviewed may tell stories of family reunions and occasions of celebration of cultural membership; the young may write counter-stories that reflect their views (perhaps unfavourable, ambivalent or openly resistant) of such occasions.

Family Stories from Lord Dufferin School

We were fortunate to be part of a two-year project at an inner-city school in Toronto, where story became the focus of the students' work just as Shirley Brice Heath has outlined. The idea for building a storytelling project with the whole school was coordinated by a teacher, Helen Bryce, in the spring of 1997 when students, teachers and parents decided to promote the development of their skills in storytelling. Professional storytellers from different parts of the world, Bob Barton included, shared part of their culture and background with the school community. From storytelling came the story-writing stage, during 1998, when David Booth worked with the teachers connecting writing and literacy.

In the spring of 1999, students from grades 2 to 8 illustrated their particular stories under the guidance of Mark Thurman, a professional storyteller, writer and artist. This was a particularly exciting stage as Mark had himself once been a student at Lord Dufferin School.

Many of the students at this school come from countries around the world where conditions of war have sparked their move to Canada. Some of the students are first-generation born in Canada, and they collected life stories about their parents' journeys to Canada. Some students from Canadian-born families shared stories about growing up in the urban community of Regent Park. Some parents told stories to their children, who then became the storytellers. The stories may bring out different feelings of happiness or sadness, but all of them have a common message of pride and respect for the family. All the students at Lord Dufferin School and their families have important stories to tell and share. For the school's Project Review some of the students read their stories aloud to an audience of parents, community members, board officials and superintendents. As a result of this project and the publication of a book called *Family Stories from Lord Dufferin P.S.*, we are able to read the life stories of a community, a school of narratives. The following examples are drawn from the book, as are many others we have included in other chapters as support for our own work.

My Story
By Nasir Mohamud, Grade 7

In 1990, there was a war in my country Somalia. For the first time, I saw war and heard guns. One day I was in school and our house was blown up. My brother, my mom and I were lucky because we weren't there. But my aunt and one of my friends were in there and they died. So when our house blew up, we had to move to Kenya and it was peaceful down there. The last time I heard a gun was when I left my country.

After one year we came to Canada and we were lucky. But our dad was even more lucky because he didn't see the war or hear the guns. Now our country is still in a war for the past 8 years and people are still dying. I hope they stop the war and it gets peaceful like in Canada, so we could go back and see our family.

Why I Came to Canada
By Thuvaraka Ledchumykanthan, Grade 8

This story began after my father left Sri Lanka in 1990. My father came to Canada on June 2, 1990 by airplane. It was a dark night when things were becoming dangerous and things were being destroyed and my family was not safe. My mother said to my neighbours that my family wanted to be safe. We went to a bunker, a place made out of mud.

After a few days living there, my mother decided that we should go live in Colombo, the capital city of Sri Lanka, where my aunt lived. My mother said, "First let's go to Klenchi." There my mother met some of her relatives. The relatives said that they would take us to Colombo but my brother had to go with someone else. My mom asked a friend of hers if she could take my brother to Colombo with her and she said yes.

My grandmother, my brother and I got to Colombo first. Then a few months later my sister and my mother arrived. After a year living there my family decided to come to Canada. My father sponsored my family and me.

After a few months I arrived in Canada and lived in Mississauga for three years. I went to three different schools. They were Haven Wood P.S., Cherry Hill P.S. and Tomkin Road P.S.

Finally I moved to this neighbourhood, Regent Park, in September of 1996.

The Hungry Alligator
By Sandy Sukraj, Grade 4

Many, many years ago, when my grandfather was still alive, he used to work in the canals near the sugar cane fields in Guyana. He and his partner used to work very hard cleaning the weeds and grass out of the canals.

No people lived back in and around the fields and there was no access to transportation or anything else. So every morning, trucks would come around to take everyone to work and then take them all back home in the evening.

One day, my grandfather went to work with the other men as usual. He worked all day and when it was almost time to go home, he had just a small area in the canal to clean out. The rest of the workers were finished their jobs and were getting ready to head for the trucks when they heard my grandfather screaming in fear and pain.

They rushed to the water and found an alligator attacking him. As they pulled him out, the angry alligator pranced around. My poor grandfather nearly died that day. He was bleeding a lot from all his wounds. When the truck arrived, he was taken to the hospital.

Grandfather couldn't walk for weeks and he was scared for a long time from his experience but he was thankful to be still alive.

Coming to Canada
By Van Quan Phu, Grade 7

My mom and I came to Canada because back in Vietnam we were poor and because my aunt, uncle, grandmother and grandfather lived in Canada. My mom swore that if she could make it over to Canada she would cut her hair bald.

It all started when my mom, aunt and uncle and I left Vietnam on a boat. There were a lot of people, about 40, so we had to eat less. When we got onto the Ocean there were storms and lightning. At the time I was only 2 years old. My aunt and uncle thought they were going to die. My uncle got a rope so he, my mom, my aunt and I could tie our hands together so that if we died and floated to land people would bury us together.

But the next morning, the storm and lightning stopped. We were so happy that we hadn't died. We went to Singapore and we were separated from my aunt and uncle. We lived there for a while. Then the people from Canada came to test people to see if they knew how to speak English, but my mom failed. They sent us to the Philippines. My mom and I stayed there for 4 years. By then, my mom had my two year old brother and a sister, just born.

Soon after, the people from Canada came again. This time my mom passed and they sent us to Canada. The church people took care of us. They gave us food and clothing. They asked if we wanted to live in a church in Mississauga. My mom said no because by then my aunt, uncle, grandmother and grandfather lived in Toronto. She wanted to be near them. The people helped us to get a house to live in because we didn't have a father and this is where we live now.

The Last Vacation Event
By Nisa Mullaithilaga, Grade 5

After school was over in 1993, I was only 6 years old. I just found out that we were going to 4 different places that we had never been to out of Toronto. The places were: London; to see my uncle, aunt, and my baby cousin, Germany; to see my three uncles, three aunts, and a grandmother, Switzerland; to see my aunt and cousin, and Paris; to see my uncle. We went with my grandmother, my mother and my brother.

The thing I hate is that my father is never able to attend because he has some kind of job to take care of. Whenever we go on a trip and my father has a job to take care of I would start to cry.

When we were going to Switzerland we met our aunt and my cousin.

After a few days passed, we had to go to the food market. Around us were hundreds of stores and we looked at each and every store. When we went to our second store, I was walking ahead. I was walking straight but my mom took a left turn. When I looked behind me I saw no one except people that I didn't know. I looked all over and couldn't find a trace of my mother and a few minutes later I started to cry.

An old woman came up to me and asked why I was crying. I told her what happened and she brought me to the security station. They asked me my name and told me to wait outside. A few minutes later I saw my mom and I ran up to her and gave her a huge bear hug.

From that day on whenever we're out of Toronto, I stay beside my mom no matter what. I've always wondered how it would feel if I had stayed lost in Switzerland for my entire lifetime. But lucky for me that old woman helped me.

I also wondered that if my father had been there, I probably wouldn't have gotten lost because when I try holding his hand he plays around. I would still be with him and paying attention to the games we would be playing with our hands and not have gotten lost.

A Story About My Parents
By Anita Alaguajan, Grade 2

In January 1987, my dad left Sri Lanka to come to Canada. When he came to Toronto, he lived at 142 Wellesley St. My dad had two jobs; one in the day and one in the night.

During the day he worked at a car company. At night he worked in a knitting factory making socks. My dad met my mom in the sock factory. She worked there too.

On August 28, 1989, my dad and mom got married. On April 12, 1990, I was born. That was a happy day for my mom and dad.

Story Goes to School

...if certain stories are never heard beyond a narrow circle – for example, if stories of toughness are never echoed or challenged in stories heard in the classroom forum – they will never be "dialogized," to use Bakhin's term. That is, they will not be rendered a story among possible stories, other ways of being; in which case, they may be a source of identification and power of constraint, of limits.

Anne Dyson and Cecilia Genishi,
The Need for Story

School life is full of all sorts of contexts for story-making. The children live inside a story culture of gossip in the cloakroom, retellings of television shows, games and songs at recess, anecdotes about what happened on the weekend when they saw their teacher eating in a restaurant. We know that children have heard hundreds of stories before they come to school, family stories that are told over and over again, stories from the playground, television and relatives. As teachers, we can tap into these home tales and home truths, and use them to connect with other stories from other families in other times in other worlds. We can also share our own personal stories from our own lives, participating in the storying process. We must value the family stories, the recess rhymes, the urban rumours, the tall tales; they are gold spun into story and they add to our wealth as storyers.

But it is also our hope to make children strong with written stories as well, authored tales that involve the reading and writing processes. Unfortunately, this hope sometimes drive us to focus on books rather than on stories, on reading instead of on storying, on "reading comprehension" when meaning or understanding should be the outcome. How can we nurture literacy without damaging the story flowers?

It is precisely story's power to evoke images that, in the words of Penelope Farmer, "lessen the huge distances between ourselves and other people," which lies at the heart of what we mean about stories and their uses in the classroom. This idea is interestingly presented in Lois Lowry's novel, *The Giver*, where she creates a world of orderly disciplined life. Nothing is ever unexpected, inconvenient or unusual. It is a life without colour, pain or past. Jonas, the story's protagonist, has been selected by his community's council of elders to be the new Receiver of Memories, a rare selection and one of great honour. No one in his community recollects anything beyond his or her own lifetime. It will be Jonas's task to learn "all that goes beyond — all that is Elsewhere — and all that goes back and back and back."

His mentor, an old man known as the Giver, describes to him the importance of memories: "It is how wisdom comes and how we shape our future." The citizens of the community know scientific facts, the Giver tells him, but without memories these are meaningless. As the memories of his community are transmitted to Jonas by means of powerful images, profound changes come over him. The more Jonas is moved and shaken by the memories of his community, the more he finds so much of what takes place in the day-to-day life of his family and friends meaningless. He is desperate for things to change. The Giver tells him:

> "It's true that it has been this way for what seems forever. But the memories tell us that it has not always been. People felt things once. You and I have been part of that, so we know. We know that they once felt things like pride, and sorrow, and—"

> "And love," Jonas added, remembering the family scene that had so affected him.

> "The worst part of holding the memories is not the pain. It's the loneliness of it. Memories need to be shared."

Oksana Kuryliw, a school principal, centred her research around this novel. She developed a storying unit with a class of Grade 8 students.

> My study of intertextual learning began with the novel *The Giver*. This print text was used to launch the study, but as we proceeded, various texts were introduced, such as storytelling, drama and film. Each "text" (stories from family members and friends, from television programs and films) produced a variety of discussions in oral and written form. Sometimes, and only sometimes, did the personal stories connect with the novel. In *The Giver*, the author creates a fictional community where there are no storytellers. The students had a difficult time making the connections among several concepts revealed in the novel: the absence of storytellers in the novel and the role of storytellers in a society; the absence of books in the fictional community and the absence of memories. The drama work explored these connections, as the children worked in role, and examined and pondered the need for recorded story, for history, for collective memory, creating an intertextual context as they drew upon everything they knew in order to handle the dramatic conflict. As one Grade 8 student commented upon the completion of my research, "Teachers are the primary texts; they are 'The Givers.' "

Sharing Stories

When children become a village of listeners, the community's story experience is composed of each individual's contributions and these must be met with both acceptance and respect. The coming together to hear stimulating material presented by an enthusiastic teller or reader resembles a ritual initiation which reinforces the idea that each and every human being is part of the total interconnectedness of things.

As story sharers, we become all the voices we have ever heard. Each story releases the natural rhythms of language and emotion in us, and sophisticated varieties of style and originality are within each individual's abilities, at least over a period of time. Many of our encounters with stories in school are shaped by our experiences with those who are sharing the stories with us. There is a triangle formed by the children, the story and the teacher. In the past, our belief as teachers often lay in helping children find "The Truth" hidden in the text, but now we realize that in order to understand a story we must negotiate the meaning between the reader and the author. There occurs a dynamic interactive transaction, where readers begin to trust their own responses, their thoughts and feelings, and then explore and share these with others.

During our years of teaching, we have spent a great deal of time sharing stories, listening and reading together, as would a group around the campfire. There are public meanings within stories that trigger universal connections for all of us experiencing the story, as well as private meanings for each individual involved. Even the shared meanings will have private aspects, since each of us makes our own stories in our minds based on unique life experiences. However, these shared ideas unite us, join us together in common expectations and awareness. After we listen or read and experience, we can then story together, exploring our concerns, clarifying our own questions, altering our public and private stories, building story frames for "us" as well as for "me."

Much of school is individualized, and that is as it should be. A book, after all, is a one-on-one affair between author and reader. Yet if we are gathered together by clans in schoolrooms, can we not cooperate and collaborate on making new story meanings that affect all of us?

What stories hold! Words never known, yet immediately understood. Patterns of language seldom, if ever, used by the children — literary structures that carry a heritage of thought from our linguistic past, translations from other cultures rich in sound and sense, melodies and rhythms that tune the ear to the power of words (e.g., metaphors, images and analogies for making meaning from our story senses). Thirty-six children give us thirty-six times the language power of our "teacher" voices.

Children new to English find in a story context for understanding. It is not word lists that will command their attention, but the lives of the characters who fill the tales they read or listen to, both in the stories of their classmates and in the literary stories they meet. How painful it would be for those children new to English to sit day after day without feeling connected to what is happening in the classroom. And yet, through storying, how quickly they can enter the activity and make sense of what is happening, building their own versions, listening, telling, retelling; talking about, reflecting upon — responding.

We need a supportive and collaborative atmosphere where everyone sits inside the story circle and is part of the storying experience. In a shared story experience, we try to regroup the class into a "theatre mode," on the rug or with the chairs gathered together, so that the story can be presented in the strongest way possible. The children may sit around us, or we may somehow group them so there is a sense of belonging to the experience. The teacher's voice and demeanour will be part of this, and he or she has to be aware of the audience contact and of how the story is being experienced. Commercially available tapes and records to complement the teacher's own tellings and readings, readers' theatre presentations by rehearsed groups, professional storytellers, guests, student teachers and parents — they can all be part of the community of readers who celebrate storying with children.

How we approach story sharing is important to the success of the stories we read and tell. It is also important that the teacher constantly adapt the program to fit the needs of the group. In *Bringing Children and Reading Together*, Charles Reasoner asks us some significant questions:

> Do you display the book in advance so children can browse through it to see if they wish to make plans to attend? When story time is approaching, do you give children time to finish their work, a five- or ten-minute warning? Do you have them in a comfortable position? If they are sitting on the floor, is it warm enough? Is the lighting adequate? Are you standing or sitting so they have to hold their heads uncomfortably? Can the children at the back of the room see you and, if there are any, the pictures? Can you read the story a second time if the class so chooses? Do you draw attention away from the story with unnatural gestures or a voice that is loud, strained or phony? Do you talk down to young audiences? Do you patronize them? Do you tag a moral ending onto a story so that it's unnecessarily anticlimactic? Do you interrupt the story, do you break the mood, the magic, the flow for a teaching commercial or a vocabulary lesson? If a child has disturbed the story reading, do you seat him within arm's reach? Do you put off questions or anecdotes volunteered by children by shaking your head slightly or changing expression? Do you time the story so that it comes at a convenient time for children's energies, for the rhythm of the class? Do you read stories to the children they would not normally read for themselves? Do you interpret each story to its fullest? Do you relate and connect stories from one period to another so that a story repertoire emerges? Do you give children time to respond to a story?

New Stories from Old Stories

Children enjoy stories. They sense the freedom in the structure, the elixir in the container. They begin to anticipate and predict from the first moments of a story's beginning. They gather round the storyer and know that the experience will be worthwhile. There will be learning, but first there will be story, and the initial responses of children will be personal and organic. Good teachers will move children on to other learning areas, focusing the experience as the children are caught up in all of the ideas being explored. But we must be careful not to use stories solely for our own teaching goals. Story is an art form unto itself, a worthwhile experience even without teaching follow-ups. If we can enrich and extend learning with story, so much the better. In classrooms where children are exposed to a wide range of stories and books and where they are encouraged to think of themselves as authors too, the functions of reading quickly become apparent. When this kind of reading experience is reinforced through collaboration between home and school with respect to shared reading experiences, opportunities for helping children to know stories more fully and like them better are greatly enhanced.

Every time we read a story, it is created anew. We see that story from our own perspectives, using our experiences to make new sense of that story. We now see reading as a co-creative or re-creative act. As we retell a story, we re-synthesize and restate ourselves, in our present versions. By being involved in the reading experiences of others, we learn to look at our own subjective responses with some objectivity. We begin to recognize our own styles of perception, exploring others' methods of making texts mean something. Insightful and skilled teachers give young readers help in building imaginative re-creations, retelling stories in a variety of ways. Each story is raw material for children as they explore the range of possibilities in shaping their own personal and collective responses. As teachers, we must be careful to understand the sensitivity and imagination that children bring to a text, and to understand the suggestivity of a story in creating imaginative responses.

Some story worlds are easy for us to enter: we have seen that mountain, we have lived in that city, we have known those bulrushes, or we have owned a dog like the one we met in the story. Other stories are more difficult to enter: we need the artful author who invites us in, the clever storyteller who pulls us along, or the insightful teacher who builds us a shared context. As we hear or read the words, we create a set of images in our minds, we transform those symbols into startling pictures that let us see into the story.

In *The Implied Reader*, Wolfgang Iser says that the author and reader are to share the game of the imagination, and indeed the game will not work if the text sets out to be anything more than a set of governing rules. Children build up their impressions of a story as they go along "from a moving viewpoint which travels along inside that which it has to apprehend." This wandering viewpoint allows the reader to add to the possibilities that lie within this transactional mode of creation. All readers are making some kinds of meanings through their interactions. It is this dynamic of the act of storying that will allow teachers to help individual students with their own transactions with the text. As we combine literary and lived-through experiences, we make meaning with each story, and by sharing our collective meanings, we build our own stronger and bigger world. We must reassure children of the validity of their own personal reconstructions.

A Story Culture

The challenges in bringing about a story culture in the classroom are many, but so are the strategies. As teachers, we need to care about the stories we use, realizing the powerful effect of narrative on children. When they hear the story we read or tell, they listen to the heartbeats of those beside them in the story circle. They are the storyteller, the story and the listener, all in one.

In a colleague's drama classroom, the Grade 7 gifted students entered for their weekly drama class, took their seats quietly and put their heads on their desks in some strange, silent ritual. The skilled teacher gently probed for the reason for this, and the children revealed that the librarian had completed her reading of *Flowers for Algernon*, and the children, deeply moved, began to question the morality in giving and then taking intelligence from a mentally challenged man. Gradually, the students discussed all aspects of schooling for all types of people, including the problems that arose because of their segregation as "gifted" children. The story had become theirs, and they needed to story to put it in perspective, to add it to their story data base. The emotion created by the reading had to be dealt with, processed, understood. The children needed to use their own stories to make sense of the novel, and vice versa.

The Teacher's Voice

Does the classroom teacher's own use of story and language affect the students? How important are our own skills in speaking and listening, reading and writing? What types of language behaviour do we exhibit with our students during our time with them? Do the students learn from us an unwritten curriculum in languaging by simply observing, interacting with and listening to us?

If it is true that the most valuable language learning happens when students are intellectually and emotionally involved, then shouldn't it be true for the teacher as well? While the story for the teacher and the story for children may be different, the language needs of both remain constant: to communicate appropriately and effectively and to understand enough to become involved in the making of meaning, both private and public. The teacher, freed from the traditional patterns of classroom interaction, will be able to use different patterns of language in storytelling.

Of course, our use of language can have a powerful effect on the children. The teacher must read aloud, if not with the skills of a trained voice, at least with an understanding of what is being read and with a determination to read it with integrity and commitment. We need to put words and spoken language to efficient use, selecting carefully, powerfully and economically the words that best fit the purpose we put them to. Because story is a particular way of learning, the teacher must be very sensitive to language when telling a story, so that as much as possible can be revealed at any moment. As well, it is important to develop a good ear for language effect, a wide range of tone, effective volume and pitch. This sounds challenging, but take heart! The children will lead us to the language. By working alongside them, by trying on different roles and voices in the safety of the story experience, and by becoming passionately involved in the actions and reactions of the children, any teacher can learn with the children. We did, and we continue to do so.

The teacher's personal languaging abilities are important after the storytelling as well. We should be able to help rework the class talk about the story where necessary — elevating, elaborating, extending, focusing, altering the mood or the tone and always, in a supportive manner, encouraging the participation of the children and honing the quality of their language and thought. The art of language is the heart of teaching. Story is one medium that deeply values the language of both teacher and student. It provides an opportunity for us as teachers to learn along with the children, and lets us share in their exploration of language.

We have seen teachers of all types sharing stories — first-time student teachers, teachers with forty years' experience, teachers with voice training from Royal Academies, teachers who could hardly be heard, teachers who had never heard a story told, teachers who read what their teachers had read, teachers too tired to stand, teachers wearing a storytelling apron, teachers drawing children into a tale, teachers reading from the safety of a lectern, teachers who found a story accidentally, teachers with libraries that would shame us — and in every case, if the story was given honestly, with belief and commitment, the children listened, and often begged for more. Whenever a principal entered our classrooms years ago and caught us reading to the class, we would grow embarrassed or defensive; now we invite the administration in to listen, to laugh, to join in, even to share a story of his or her own. Such are the changes in our lives since story went to school. Dick, Jane, Puff, Spot and Baby Sally have been rescued by truth, tears, laughter and empathy. Mother has been freed from scrubbing the floor in her good dress, and Father has abandoned his tie and his fedora. Story is here, and it is powerful. It is "us."

Teacher Stories

Narrative can help us as teachers to look at our professional selves from the inside out, as we describe and reflect upon our experiences in and out of the classroom, constructing and giving form to the events of our teaching lives, stories both for ourselves and for sharing with others. Storytelling from our teaching lives can help us to see the commonalties in our different situations, and to realize that other teachers face problems similar to ours, and feel the same satisfaction from teaching successes. Finding out that other teachers ask themselves questions about professional practice draws us together in the teaching community. Constructing our own narratives and sharing the narratives of our colleagues may alter our teaching forever, as we come to see ourselves and others through different lenses.

Andy Anderson, a teacher/educator, demonstrated this effectively when he told this story at a conference for new teachers:

Early in my teaching career I was a physical and health educator at a rural elementary school near Stratford. To encourage participation in vigorous physical activity I had set up a running course through a nearby sugar bush that was owned by one of families whose children attended our school. The marked courses ranged in distance and level of challenge. Each time I brought a class to the bush for a run I would jog along with one of the students. On one of these occasions I was running with a young, twelve- or thirteen-year-old Mennonite boy named Harley. His buttoned-up, long-sleeved shirt, long pants and well-worn, flat-soled Converse running shoes comprised his "gym" uniform. As we ran along I entertained discussion about a number of topics: school, sports, his interests, etc. Noticing the pace I was setting was not very difficult for Harley I decided to pick up speed. Again, no visible signs of strain and Harley kept on talking. I increased the pace to a level I now was finding intense. I had stopped talking half a kilometre ago. Harley was striding along beside me effortlessly. When we finished the course and I caught my breath I said to Harley, "Have you ever thought about coming out for cross-country running?" He indicated he had chores after school each night and so could not attend practices unless they were at school. I agreed to find ways for him to practice if he would agree to come to the cross-country meet in mid-October. One of Harley's training programs consisted of chasing down cows. Each night he had to round up cattle with the farm dog. Invariably some strayed or were contrary. Harley would run after the animals until they had been corralled or returned to the herd. It was classic interval training. It was apparent Harley loved to run. His distance pace was not much different from his sprint. His aerobic capacity was uncommon. The cross-country meet was held at a conservation area near London. The course runs through wooded areas with some steep hills and winding territory among evergreens and a stream. As the competitors and their entourage arrived both Harley and I looked out of place. As a rookie teacher from one of those country schools I had no credibility. Harley didn't have the tracksuit to ceremoniously remove in preparation for the start. Also he could not sport the school colours. His uniform was again the buttoned-up shirt, long pants and now well-worn Converse runners. What is a kid in street clothes doing among the prestige athletes? My advice to Harley was simple: "Stay close to the leaders, don't let them squeeze you back in the pack, after you reach the halfway point listen to how you feel and let your body tell you whether to speed up or hang on, but most of all enjoy the run.

The gun sounded and the runners headed off in a pack: the coaches then readied the shute for their return. The shute funnelled the runners through to the finish so we could tabulate the results in some coherent fashion. Nervously we all paced the finish area. Suddenly one of the field marshals signaled the first group of runners was approaching the top of the hill that overlooked the route to the finish. Although we could not distinguish who the runners were, we could without a doubt distinguish their colours — the school they represented. One of the coaches turned to his colleagues and shouted, "It's some kid in street clothes out front."

Now it was my turn to squirm my way through to the front of the line to scream and wave, "Come on Harley, RUN, RUN!! As he entered the shute I could tell he had had the time of his life. He said he tried to talk to some people during the race but nobody would talk back so he kept moving ahead to the next person. Finally when there was nobody left he said he just let go and started to run his best. I was so proud of him. Harley taught me a lot about teaching and coaching. It's not whether you win or lose but how you play the game, not just how you play the game strategically but how you enjoy the game/race for the love of being involved in this moment of peak experience, how you experience this joy of movement and the flow and fluidity of mind, body and soul, and unless as teachers we take the time to run along beside our learners listening to them with our eyes and ears, heads and hearts, we may never get to know our learners and the important possibilities in their lives.

Teachers' Stories as Research

If story is a basic way of organizing experience, and if we search for our own stories in the stories of others, can narrative be a form of research that we can employ to examine education and our role in the teaching/ learning process? Florence Samson, coordinator of practice teaching at the University of Toronto, decided to explore this storying issue from her own doctoral thesis, "Teacher Story/Student Story: Teacher Voice/ Student Voice."

During that first term of doctoral studies, I struggled to unearth, articulate and understand my stories of experience. I also searched for answers to my never-ending and ever-nagging questions about the value of narrative inquiry as a research methodology. My traditional perceptions and stories of research were challenged. The journey to completion of the dissertation was, for me, a catalyst to a life of awakenings and transformations for we live and tell our lives through story and in the telling and retelling of our stories we learn new ways of being. We also learn new ways of teaching and learning for "stories lived and told educate the self and others, including the young and those, such as researchers, who are new to their communities…"

This affirmation, however, was accompanied by an unexpected and sometimes unwelcome challenge, for narrative inquiry turned the tables on me and forced me to go to my own experience, to where I was as a teacher. In the process of coming to understand my teaching, I realised that I had to look beyond my performance in the classroom, to search more deeply inside myself, to go inward and outward, backward and forward in order to articulate my teacher story and listen to my teacher voice. In time I came to understand that the life experience which I bring to the classroom determines how I behave in the classroom. In order to understand my teaching, I had to come to understand my experience. I, therefore, learned to story and re-story my experiences and examine the contexts in which they were lived. Although I was unaware at the time, my stories of teaching and living were sometimes "cover" stories, not the stories which were deep inside-the "secret" stories of what it was to be a woman and a teacher. Certain topics were private and not for sharing. As teachers and women we did not talk about the things which displeased us or interfered with society's images of the good teacher and the good woman. I now realise that in our acceptance we unknowingly submerged our questions, our doubts and our fears. We became complicit in the silencing of our own voices and our secret stories remained hidden, untold and unrecorded. On the outside, I told and continued to cling to the accepted and expected stories. On the inside, like many other women of my 1960s generation, I was frustrated in trying to be all that I wanted to be and all that I was expected to be — the best mother, best wife, best teacher, best church worker. I struggled to integrate the stories I felt inside and the stories I lived in public. I was pulled in many directions in trying to live my story of teacher and woman. Narrative methodology gives us permission to make our individual and collective experiences at home and at school visible by inviting us to name these experiences. In doing so we move from the isolation that is often experienced personally and professionally into relationship and community. Without the articulation of our stories and the discovery of resonance and relationship, we live in personal and professional isolation. It is in making time to come together that we ensure the sharing of stories and the subsequent personal and professional development.

Telling Stories to Children

Mouth Open Story Jump Out

Mouth open story jump out I tell you me secret
you let it out
But I don't care if the world hear shout it out
Mouth open story jump out
Besides, the secret I tell you wasn't even true so you can shout till you blue
So boo mouth open story jump out

John Agard

Storytelling may be the oldest of all the arts. The mother told the story to her child, the hunter to his peers, the survivor to his rescuers, the priestess to her followers, the seer to his petitioners. The better the tale was told, the more it was believed and remembered. When we read or tell a story aloud, we release it from the printed page, we give it life. Our role is to let the story "jump out."

There are characteristics, however, which contribute to a story's success and these should be kept in mind. Plot unity is all-important. Look for a beginning, a middle and an end containing an action so that no matter how unpredictable the episodes might be, the story binds them together in such a way that the listener is delighted. A story such as "Rapunzel" is a worthy example.

Stories that are told in close logical sequence, that avoid a lot of extraneous clutter (talking around the issues and flashing forward or back) are stories that give satisfaction to the listener.

We can't all tell the same stories. There are some we are drawn to immediately and others which just don't seem to succeed. Stories are invaluable to the teacher because they permit the child time to daydream; they let the mind wander; they sharpen perception and the reflective processes.

It is not necessary to change the words to suit the age level of the audience. The imagination of the child and the context of the story usually supply the keys to understanding. Many of the more difficult words contribute atmosphere by their mere sound; it doesn't always matter what they mean. As author Joan Aiken writes in *"On Imagination,"* "Things not understood have a radiance of their own."

Continued exposure to stories may develop in children an understanding of structure so they can predict what new stories they would like. They will come to expect a definite beginning, middle and ending; they will come to expect the resolution of a problem which will leave them feeling satisfied; they will develop an understanding of characters and situations, thus providing them with a kind of story shorthand for dealing with complex notions such as selfishness, wickedness or deceit.

There are always reactions from listeners that reveal something about the story that the storyteller may not have noticed or known. By watching the listeners, a teacher can come to a new understanding, and he or she and the class can have a new and enriching experience. The pleasure that arises between speaker and listener rests on the teller's interpretation, which may — or may not — stimulate the listener's imagination to set the scene, visualize the players and follow the action. The voice, expression, gestures and imagination of the storyteller are powerful factors in determining whether the audience experiences a story vividly and creatively. If the teacher is enthusiastic about a story and sincerely motivated to tell it, genuine success with storying will likely follow.

Storytelling in the Classroom

Bob Barton writes:

Picture one hundred and fifty Grade 8 boys crowding into a tiny assembly hall, each one endeavouring to win a spot against the back wall. (That's about as far away from the storytelling bloke as one can get.) Now picture several distraught teachers attempting to redistribute boys about the room. Eventually order is restored and the boys are seated. Although the room is small and tightly packed the boys have managed to leave a yawning chasm between themselves and the teller, me.

The year is 1998 and I'm told that I'm the first storyteller these boys have met. I try to break the ice and ask, "What do you think a storyteller does?"

The reply is swift and sure, "Tells stories to little kids."

I explain that I have probably told more stories to adults than to children and I try to get them thinking about themselves as storytellers. They aren't buying, so I launch quickly into a story. The room grows still.

The teachers talk afterwards about inviting a storyteller more often and about the benefits and pleasures of coming together in shared activity of this nature.

It is good for students to come together to share as a community. But even more important I think is the opportunity storytelling offers for sustained listening and listening is a skill which has been very much overlooked in the overall scheme of things lately.

As a professional storyteller who works mainly in schools, I often regret that I don't have the opportunity to do more by way of exploration with the stories. I come into the school such as the one I've just described. I tell my stories. I leave. Perhaps there is some context for my visit. Perhaps the work with story continues but I don't think this is always the case.

During the early part of this century there were concerted attempts to encourage the development of storytelling in education. It's interesting to note the numbers of books for teachers that were published in the twenties, thirties and forties. Unfortunately, from the 1950s on, storytelling gradually fell victim to powerful competition from film, television and computers.

It seems ironic these days, when storytelling's potential goes largely unrecognized in schools, that it is making rapid advances in the adult community. From the rise of adult storytelling festivals in the late seventies, storytelling has continued to make inroads into the adult entertainment scene. A recent article in the *New York Times* (May 2, 1999) describes an evening at the Moth Bar in New York City as "one of the phenomena of storytelling as entertainment that is gaining momentum nationwide. The evening draws on the traditions of professional yarnspinners who tend to tell and retell the same stories, often fable-like in tone. In the past, such tellers were hired by schools to recount stories to pupils. Now they find themselves in cafe and bars regaling adults."

An interesting thought just crossed my mind. Wouldn't it be great a few years from now, if those Grade 8 boys I described earlier were found beating down the door of a bar somewhere in order to get in to listen to a storyteller? Now that would be sweet.

Preparing to Tell Stories

Telling a story is not a difficult task to master, especially if you begin with a simple repetitive or cumulative tale. A story by Linda Williams called *The Little Old Lady Who Wasn't Afraid of Anything* makes a good example. The plot is simple: a little old lady goes into the woods to collect nuts and berries and seeds. She stays too late and is overtaken by night. As she rushes along the path home she encounters a pair of clomping boots, wriggling trousers, a flapping shirt, two white gloves, a tall black hat and eventually a large, scary jack-o'-lantern. All chase the old woman to her house, where she barricades herself behind locked doors. But she is the little old lady who isn't afraid of anything, isn't she? How she handles her dilemma is both clever and funny.

Because the story is repetitive and cumulative and supports prediction, the telling of it invites much chiming in. For example, each encounter with objects ("Right in the middle of the path were two big shoes") is followed by a description of the noise the objects make ("and the shoes went CLOMP, CLOMP"). Each time the old woman flees from an object the words, "But behind her she could hear. . ." are repeated. Ever so slight a pause each time the teller approaches these bits of the story never fails to elicit the vocal predictions of the listeners.

As the children get caught up in the mystery and fun, chiming in with known bits, their confidence grows and the story, borne on the playful and imaginative interchange between teller and audience, comes to life. By listening to intonation, pause, pitch, rhetoric and the sympathetic response of the human voice to the rhythms of language, children quickly build a story repertoire which, if it becomes the stuff of their reading, is like visiting old friends. Simultaneously they come to understand what to expect of a story's structural pattern, conventions and connections to the world of storytelling.

A question frequently asked of storytellers is, "Do you tell the story the way it is in the book?" There are probably as many answers to that question as there are storytellers, for how a story is brought to life is central to storytelling. Certainly it is essential that the storyteller remain faithful to the core of the story, but how each person embellishes the story is what makes storytelling such an exciting art-form. This approach may be useful:

- After reading the story once, slowly, make an outline of it in your own words and then try telling it to yourself.
- A second reading of the story will reveal if any significant details have been omitted.
- Read the story a third time and consider the feelings and attitudes of the story characters. Try telling it to yourself again.
- On the fourth reading pay close attention to the language of the story. What words or phrases should be preserved to retain the story's unique sound? Tell the story again to yourself.
- A fifth reading might be devoted to blocking the story into scenes and considering the sensory details (sights, sounds, colours, etc.). Now tell the story to yourself again.
- A final reading should concentrate on the beginning and ending. A strong start and a confident finish are important: you may want to memorize the beginning and ending of the story. There are various editing techniques that might also be employed (e.g., condensing the story; elaborating on something only hinted at; dropping an extraneous character; converting dialogue to narrative or vice versa; rearranging the plot, especially if the story's exposition is too long; experimenting with the narrative style). Insight into the kind of shaping a story requires becomes more apparent after you have told yourself the story a few times.
- The real test of your telling comes when you face your audience. Storytelling is an audience-valuing situation. The storyteller should feel the audience response throughout and continually modify the delivery accordingly. The important thing is to start slowly, watch carefully the responses of your listeners, and maintain your concentration. See your story, feel it — make everything happen. Use the voice you use in everyday conversation and respond naturally to your feelings about the story. As for gestures and body language, let

them be natural as well. With practice you will quickly learn what is right for your own style and delivery.

Participating in the Story

Some teachers gain more confidence telling a story when they actively involve the children in some way:

- Choose a story that features repetition of certain words or phrases or has a refrain. Once the students know how the story is working, a pause by the teller is all the invitation they need to join in.
- Catalogue all the sound effects that will be required by a story (e.g., wind on a stormy night; footsteps on a creaking floor; rain on a tin roof; cats yowling on a back fence, etc.). Rehearse the sounds together and establish a signal system so the students will know when to contribute or halt the sound. Tell the story and have the students add the right sounds in the appropriate places.
- Find a story with repeated dialogue between or among characters. The students can be given roles as one or more of the characters and the story can be told in call and response fashion between teller and listener. ("There's a hole in the bucket" is a good example.)
- With a simple direct story featuring few characters and a repetitive plot, the teller might employ a drama technique known as "voice-over narration." The teller relates the tale, and the students, all working in their own space, enact the actions of the central characters or characters in mime or movement. (Try "The Brahmin, the Tiger and the Jackal," a folktale from India.)

Reading Aloud to Children

Some stories we know so well that we read them as if we were telling them from our hearts. The stories that we try to choose to read are those that we enjoy ourselves. Every time we share one with a group of children, we find new meanings to interpret aloud. It may be a word with a delicious sound, a dialogue in which we can employ different voices, a mood that can be created with careful modulation, a feeling conjured up by the artful magic of the writer. As you become familiar with a story, you will find yourself maintaining eye contact with the children, sensing their responses so that you can build upon them. If you are using a picture book, then the illustrations are telling the story as well. How important that the children have an opportunity to notice the father and the children in Anthony Browne's *Piggybook* turning literally into pigs, or the similarity of the father and the gorilla in Browne's *Gorilla*. Sometimes, the pictures can be saved for a second reading, so that the story is uninterrupted the first time. Children can use the illustrations later for their own storytelling of both literary and personal anecdotes.

With young adolescents it is often thought that stories must necessarily be fast-paced and tinged with gore to capture this seemingly complacent audience. Adolescents may appear worldly on the outside, but deep down they want to learn about life's complexities. Stories emphasizing human relationships are important to them, but the material mustn't be preachy or didactic. Like all of us, they respond to a good yarn. Don't overlook folktales with these youngsters. This may be exactly the time in their lives when these stories will really connect with them. At the conclusion of storytelling or reading aloud there may be no need to introduce a follow-up activity. Letting the story settle into the landscape of individual imagination may be quite sufficient. If the children keep talking about the story or seem to need further involvement with aspects of it, then capitalize on it. Occasionally a longer story which is being presented serially over a number of days may require some extra attention, especially if there are gaps of a day or more between sessions or if the story is slow to hook the listeners. Reading a special novel aloud over a period of time can develop anticipation and speculation if the children are enjoying the experience. Choose a novel of depth, one that they might not choose, and build on it upon completion as a unit or theme of study.

A Novel Unit

Following is a summary of how one teacher introduced William Mayne's novel *Kelpie* to her Grade 4 class. Before reading to her students the teacher conducted the following activities:

- The students worked in pairs and labeled themselves A or B.
- The As made a body or vocal sound. The Bs, with eyes closed, told their partners what the sound reminded them of. (They were not to identify how their partner was creating the sound.)
- The students worked as a large group, each student in his or her space.
- The teacher introduced a series of sounds.
- The students replied with a movement for each.
- The teacher made a series of movements.
- The class responded with a sound.
- The teacher explained that very ordinary things can be made to appear mysterious…such as some of the sounds and activities in the exercises.
- The students in groups of six were now asked to create tableaux of a forest. The forest was to look and sound mysterious.
- The tableaux were arranged in a circle. The teacher stood in the centre and slowly pointed around the circle from left to right. As the teacher's finger pointed at them the tableaux were to be still and sounds created. In this way participants were both spectators and actors in the activity.

The teacher then introduced the novel itself, about a class outing in which the students believe a water horse (kelpie) is inhabiting a lake. "Mysterious and ordinary is very much at the heart of this story. Let's listen to the first chapter."

At the conclusion of the chapter, the teacher asked the students to describe images they had formed in their minds as they listened.

Next they were asked to recreate one story image in their minds and describe it to a partner.

In discussion afterward the teacher encouraged the students to talk about their mental images. "Did anything seem out of the ordinary? Have you ever seen anything like this? What sound might you have heard if you were there?"

The students were asked to think of a title for the first chapter. In doing this they were encouraged not only to think about what they had heard, but to predict what the novel might be about. Many of the students said that they thought the story was very much like a fantasy.

Chapter Two, dealing with the class outing, was read the following day. At the conclusion of the reading, the children were organized into five groups. Each group was assigned a story character. The groups were asked to discuss what their character would probably say about the class outing. When groups had considered all the things their character might say, each group member, in role as the character, took a turn sharing a memory of the class outing with the others.

The teacher explained that a parent had heard about strange goings on in the class outing and complained to the local school inspector. She would now take the role of the school inspector and conduct an investigation. The students were to remain in character in their groups. When addressed by the inspector any member of the group representing that character could take a turn replying.

At their next meeting, the teacher read chapters Three and Four. The teacher invited a student to play the role of the scientist who was famous for tracking down apparent sightings of water monsters in the Scottish Lochs. The student sat in a chair at the head of the class. Students in pairs were invited in turn to stand behind the scientist and discuss sightings or stories they had heard about the water horse.

At the conclusion of the stories, the scientist was to confirm or deny the talk that had taken place behind his/her back. The students were also able to question the scientist further.

At the completion of this activity the teacher asked the students if anything in these early chapters made a pattern. This discussion led the children into a great deal of anticipating about the chapter to come.

At this point, the teacher passed out copies of the novel and let the students continue reading by themselves. Interest was so high that the students couldn't wait to read to the end.

The Courage to Read Aloud

Daniel Pennac has written *Better than Life*, an entertaining, yet poignant book addressing the problem of the lack of desire to read among many children, teenagers and adults in our society. We sense the frustrations in the child as he tries to resolve the Herculean task of reading four hundred pages and then writing a report due the following day, and the frustration of his parents who can't understand why their son no longer likes to read — after all, he used to love reading when he was younger — and the teacher's seemingly fruitless attempts to try to instil a love of reading in his students. Sitting in front of television sets, parents extol the virtues of reading and blame their children's lack of desire to read on the distractions of malls, a consumer society, outdated school programs, teachers and the electronic invasion of television, stereos and computers.

Before children can read for themselves, parents spend time reading stories to them, allowing them to create wonderful imaginary worlds. Children come to know their favourite stories and never seem to tire of hearing these stories. They become eager to learn to read themselves. For Pennac, this is where the breakdown begins. This period of storytelling is, for the child, a sacred time, but for parents it becomes another daily routine they have to make time for. And when children start school, parents stop reading. After all, school will teach them how to read, freeing the parents from the daily chore. Children can now read their own stories.

Pennac argues that for many youngsters, learning to read at school becomes a chore. It is no longer pleasure, but work. It becomes homework, and there will be no television until the homework is done. Thus, television is lifted to the status of a reward, and reading is degraded to a chore that must be completed before the reward is granted. Books are no longer a floating journey of pleasure, but a battle of strange words and syllables — the freedom of fantasy lost to the struggle with fact. Pennac believes that in order to combat this aversion students have to books, parents and educators need to start reading aloud to them again, to start becoming storytellers again.

A Story Classroom

Three golden apples fell from heaven... one for the storyteller, one for the listener, and one for the one who heard.

Armenian Proverb

When the children in Larry Swartz's Grade 4 and 5 classroom entered the room on the first day of school they were greeted by a display of thirty picture books from his classroom library collection that filled the shelves along the front wall of the room. Larry was beginning the year with a humour theme, and after discussing with the children what makes stories funny, he distributed one picture book to each student. Such authors as Dav Pilkey, David Shannon, Anthony Browne, Sheree Fitch and Bernard Most were being introduced to the students within one hour of returning to school. The students spent some time reading the books silently and then together discussed the merits of each book and whether it could be considered funny or not. A few students gave a brief retelling of the stories they had read and then the students were given a Reading Response journal in which, they were told, they would be recording their thoughts about the books that they would be reading throughout the year. Larry explained to the students that the journal was a place to discuss in writing what they liked, what they didn't like, what they were reminded of, what puzzled them and what questions they might have about the books they'd be reading. He told them that he would give them some suggestions and questions that would help them use the journal effectively.

To help structure the first entry, Larry wrote two questions on the board.

1. How did you enjoy the story?
2. How did the author and illustrator of the book tickle your funny-bone?

Larry collected the journals of those who wished to submit them at this time, and began to write messages back to the students by making comments and raising questions in their journals. For one thing the students would quickly realize that their journal would have an audience and for another there was an opportunity for dialoguing about literature. Booktalk had begun. On the second day of school, Larry once again distributed a new picture book to each student. This time, before reading the books, the students were told to imagine that they were going to be judges for a funny book contest and over the next few days they would decide which books were their favourites. The whole class discussed what criteria they would use to judge their books, as Larry recorded their points on the chalkboard. For the second activity with these picture books, the students were divided into groups of five. This time, after the children read their books silently, they each presented their books to the rest of the group, perhaps retelling the story, referring to a particularly funny picture, or giving an opinion on what appealed or didn't appeal to them. Larry was able to join in on three out of the six book conferences.

The third day began with Larry sharing the book *Pete's a Pizza* by William Steig with the whole class to demonstrate some of the things that might be discussed in groups. Together the class discussed favourite illustrations such as one of Pete's father putting red checkers on Pete's stomach to add tomatoes to the pizza. The children also shared stories about special times when they played with their mothers and fathers. Some told stories about things that they remembered about pretend play when they were younger. Natasha told the class about how she used to imagine her basement was a castle and Michael told how he pretended he had an imaginary dog as a friend. During the discussion, the class compared the book to other stories about children playing that they were reminded of such as *Come Away from the Water, Shirley* by John Burningham and *No, David!* By David Shannon. To promote further reflection, Larry asked the class why they thought Pete's father was playing the pretend game with his son. He also asked the students how William Steig made the situation of pretending to be a pizza humorous. By taking the time to discuss illustrations, vocabulary and style, the students were given a model of discussing their own books back in their groups.

Each group was told that they would have to spend time choosing one book that they thought would be a suitable finalist for the funny book contest. The criteria, still displayed on the board, could be used as a reference for their decisions. If it was difficult to choose one book, they would have to consider how a decision could be reached.

After a fifteen-minute discussion, each group reported its favourite selection. The finalists were:

The Dumb Bunnies Go to the Zoo by Dav Pilkey
A Bad Case of the Stripes by David Shannon
Pete's a Pizza by William Steig
Parts by Todd Arnold
Lilly's Purple Plastic Purse by Kevin Henkes
Willy the Dreamer by Anthony Browne

Over the next week, Larry read aloud one of the selections each day so that the whole class could experience the six selections. During the week all the picture books were made available to students to choose as they wished as other activities on the humour theme were introduced into the program. As for the contest, after all six books were shared, a ballot was given to each student and a "winner" was declared. An activity such as this that has the students discussing books introduces and promotes the type of learning atmosphere that Larry intends to build in his classroom.

A Story Curriculum

If we step back and examine our own adult storying lives, we discover that narrative is indeed part of all our thought. Accepting this, we can no longer dismiss storytelling and story reading merely as effective tools in approaching "real" writing and reading. We must take seriously Harold Rosen's proposal that we look at the whole school curriculum from the point of view of its narrative possibilities. Narrative must become a more acceptable way of saying, writing, thinking and presenting. We're proposing not that anecdote should drive out analysis, but that narrative should be allowed its honourable place in the analysis of everything.

As she entered her final year of teaching, Vivian Gussin Paley tells in her book *The Girl Who Loved the Colour Brown* the story of her own farewell, along with the story of Reeny, a little girl with a fondness for the colour brown and a passion for the books of Italian author Leo Lionni. Paley and her co-teacher turned their curriculum over to a study of Lionni stories, and her students blossomed with insight, building a true 'narrative community' within a story curriculum.

What can a story do for a particular curriculum area? Consider in social science a topic such as the pioneer or immigrant. While some children copy blackboard notes, others are reading *Sarah Plain and Tall* or *Brothers of the Heart*, or listening to the teacher reading Ann Turner's *Dakota Dugout*, in which a grandmother tells her granddaughter what it was like to live in a sod house on the Dakota prairie a century ago. Perhaps Ann Turner's book *Heron Street*, about the encroachment of humans on nature as "civilization" sweeps across the country, would give children a sense of history. As Turner writes:

> I am drawn to the underside of history, the parts of the story that are prettied up and changed. We like to fix our history up a little — airbrush it so that it is somehow softer, misted with bravery and heroism, instead of full of the flaws of being human — poor decisions, silly arguments, fateful mistakes. I want a more rounded look at the past.

Or consider *Anno's Journey* by Mitsumasa Anno, in which a character first appears on the page alone, and then on each new page the same land area is pictured as the town grows through trade and commerce, until he leaves alone on the last page: the story of history can and should be told through art, through story and song, so that the feelings of those who were here before us are part of our interpretation of the past.

Kieran Egan, in *Teaching as Storytelling*, presents an interesting model that connects all teaching to storytelling. He suggests that teachers could draw upon the power of the story form, a cultural universe, to teach any content, meaningfully and engagingly, using children's imaginations. He then designs a model of teaching that draws upon the power of the story form for embedding information in an abstract context (story) that everyone already understands. Teaching should use the story model, for "stories are wonderful tools for efficiently organizing and communicating meaning."'

In her book *Creating Integrated Curriculum*, Susan Drake creates a "story model" as a means for integrating a school's curriculum with personal growth and social change built around the structure of story.

A Giant Knight

Some stories require extensive consideration before reading in order to overcome difficulties which might get in the way of understanding or enjoyment. In one classroom, a teacher wishing to use Donald Carrick's *Harald and the Giant Knight* with his Grade 4 pupils as an introduction to a theme on knights and castles thought it important that the children understand that one of the significant differences between life in medieval times and life today for the ordinary person centred on the opportunity to make choices. He created a situation where the children taking the roles of medieval peasants were able to discover the relationship between themselves and the landholding barons who were their landlords. In the course of this exploration, the children also made important discoveries about the societal functions of knights of the time. By the time they came to the story, the children were able to identify strongly with the plight of young Harald and his parents, who were faced with severe life-threatening problems when the knights from the baron's castle took over their fields during spring planting in order to carry out their battle training.

Reading Inside, Outside and All Around the Story

But if there is no teacher in there constantly encouraging, probing, pushing, delighting and challenging kids to read widely and deeply within and beyond their immediately perceived horizons, who will do it?

Paul Brock,
Teaching Literature

If children are to learn from a story, they must be able to express their individual personal concerns, ideas and feelings about it. The teacher's role is to promote thoughtful story response, to empower children to wander inside the story and wonder about it, making all kinds of meaningful connections, deepening their private and public picture of the ideas the words conjure up. The classroom can be a place where children can safely explore those connections, with the teacher as champion and lifeguard. The idea is to set up situations where the children can begin negotiating the meanings that relate the story to their lives, the author to the story, the stories that other students build to the stories in their own minds, the words that tell the story to the words that form their lives, the patterns in the story to the grammar in the head, the world of the story to the world of the moment. It is these forged links to learning that make story work worthwhile.

Designing Response Activities

As story teachers, we want to design activities that cause children to listen and read carefully, extend their knowledge, elaborate upon first understanding, invent new patterns of thought. Responding to story can be as important as meeting a story.

Teachers must be prepared to accommodate a wide range of responses to the reading. Talk, drama, painting, dance, writing, modeling, spontaneous laughter, letters to authors will be a small part of the outpouring of expression. A major plank in building a community of readers is the communal sharing of literature which has been discussed earlier. Hand in hand with this activity goes the teacher's own talk about personal reading that he or she enjoys. Teachers who read aloud with enthusiasm, who tell stories that bathe the listeners in the richness of language, are providing models of excellence for their students.

When they also share their enthusiasm for their own reading, they reinforce the models.

The Village of Round and Square Houses

Sometimes, inquiry leads us in a different direction, and instead of finding stories inside the story, a new story develops based on an incident, theme, or character from the original. What follows is a description of just such an occurrence with a class of eleven-year-olds. Their teacher had read to them *The Village of Round and Square Houses* by Ann Grifalconi. It is a true story about the village of Tos, Cameroons, West Africa, which is certainly unique in the world, for the women live in round houses and the men live in square ones. The basis of this arrangement is a story that happened to the ancestors of these people. The story involves the almost extinct volcano near which the village of Tos is situated. Contemporary rituals are an aspect of this story within a story. The remoteness of the village and the incredible difference between life there and in modern western societies is quite fascinating.

At the conclusion of the reading, the children were keen to discuss life in the remote area and to compare their own lives with the lives of children in Tos. In particular, certain daily rituals drew attention. In order to build on this interest, the teacher asked the children to invent other rituals which they thought might be practiced by the villagers of Tos. In the ensuing activity, the children invented several which related to clues they had gleaned from the story. Many of these were connected to the growing and harvesting of food.

The teacher assembled the children and announced, in role, that as a visitor to Tos she had been very impressed with the rituals and was eager to learn more. She then asked each child in turn his or her village name and also what their part in the ritual had been and what it meant to them.

At this point the teacher stopped the roleplaying and asked the children to think of some questions they might like to explore with respect to the village of Tos. The children seemed to be most interested in knowing if villagers were free to leave the village and go into the outside world. If they did do this would they be welcome to return? Could strangers visit?

It was then decided by the children that they wanted to be the outsiders first, planning to visit this village. Eventually they decided that they were scientists sent to prepare the villagers for relocation because it was feared that the volcano near which they lived would erupt again, just as it had centuries before. In groups of five, the children were to decide how they would approach the villagers with this dreadful news. Each group in turn then faced the combined groups, who represented the residents of Tos, and tried to persuade them that they must leave their ancestral lands. No group was successful in persuading the people to uproot themselves and move to a safer location. In the discussion that followed, the children decided that what would be important would be to equip the people to know when danger was imminent and help them to formulate an emergency plan which could be put into action.

Beginning with One Story

Charles Causley's twentieth-century poem "Charity Chadder," written in the style of a nursery rhyme, was the beginning of a world of stories:

> Charity Chadder borrowed a ladder,
> Leaned it against the moon,
> Climbed to the top
> Without a stop
> On the 31st of June,
> Brought down every single star,
> Kept them all in a pickle jar.

An initial reading of the text could involve the children in unison speaking, two choruses handling alternating lines. Extended work might involve identifying solo parts working in combination with chorus parts. Eventually, attempts might be made to work with different arrangements or styles, varying from upbeat and jazzy to lamenting and despairing.

Another close reading of the text might seek to identify the storyteller, the storyteller's intent and the audience for the tale. Because speculation is called for, the children can feel free to wrap the lines in a wide variety of contexts. Searching for the story's voice can produce some quite exciting interpretations. Some of the voices which one class attempted included:

- the stars themselves telling of their kidnapping and weeping over their sorry plight;
- a storyteller and chorus enjoying a call-and-response improvisation of the lines;
- Charity's girlfriends celebrating yet another fearless feat of this feckless heroine;
- anchor desk and on-site reports dealing with a crisis on the 6:00 news;
- a grandparent retelling the story of Charity's afternoon picking of blossoms from a cherry tree as an extended metaphor;
- Charity herself delivering a dramatic monologue in praise of her adventure.

Now that the text has been surrounded with a set of stories, it can be re-read with a view to seeking the stories inside. This is best achieved by encouraging the children to raise their own questions about the selection. One group of nine-year-olds asked the following:

- Why did she steal the stars?
- Why wasn't she caught?
- Was she wearing anything special at the time?
- Stars would be burning hot; how did she get them down?

- How long did it take?
- What did she do with the stars once they were in a jar?
- Did this story take place on a mountaintop?
- How did people feel about the theft?
- The stars are back now, so she must have been caught. How did this happen?
- How can the moon be protected if she strikes again?
- How did the stars get put back?

If the children are encouraged to think about their most important questions, some exciting new stories can emerge. One class wished to pursue the idea about capturing the thief. They invented amazing sky traps (how like so many ancient myths!) and a story about how Charity was captured. Another class wished to tackle the problem of returning the stars to their rightful place. Interestingly enough, rather than invoking the supernatural, they came up with a story that centred on human resourcefulness as a solution.

In one school, student teachers read the poem to all the classes on one morning, and then developed responses ranging from choral speaking to visual arts. These pictures created by the children illustrate the variety of responses that individuals had to the shared experience of the poem:

Reading beyond the story could be the next step. Throughout the world and across all cultures, human beings have told of their fearful visions of darkened skies devoid of moon and stars. A search among the world's myths could turn up dozens of stories to explain mysterious disappearances of stars or moon. Such exploration helps children to understand the interrelatedness of all the world's stories. "Charity Chadder"

may be an invention of the 1980s, but it is no more than a continuation of a story that has been told since human beings first began to tell each other stories.

In the following example, a class had just listened to the story of Theseus and the Minotaur. Identifying with mythical heroes and monsters is no mean feat. In order to bring the children into closer contact with the story, the teacher attempted to personalize it by bringing the story down to a level where the children could empathize with characters who were not actually central to the story but would be part of the background. She asked the children to think about ordinary people living long ago and to work with partners to depict in movement three tasks that might take up the time of folk living then. The children quickly came up with dozens of ideas — doing laundry, chopping wood, playing games, feeding babies, and so on. They all discussed the many ideas they had conceived. Next the children were asked to think about ordinary people living on the island of Crete during the reign of King Minos and the lifetime of the Minotaur in the Labyrinth. Once again they were to work with partners and depict three activities. This time, half the class watched while the other half performed their movement studies. Observers were instructed to find examples of what made these scenes so different from the previous ones.

In the discussion that ensued, the children indicated that they had noticed the following:

- There was much evidence of people carrying weapons while performing ordinary tasks such as harvesting, hanging up laundry, and so on.
- There was much evidence of people practicing with and caring for weapons — e.g., sharpening swords.
- Many people were depicted in attitudes of prayer.
- There was a general atmosphere of watchfulness and tension .

The teacher asked the children to sum up what they thought described the general feeling and attitude of the citizens of Crete. The children concluded: "These are people living in fear." The teacher asked the children to take this further by creating some graffiti that might have appeared on the walls of their city. The children used felt-tipped markers on large sheets of newsprint to design their graffiti, then taped their papers along one side of the classroom. The graffiti wall was an important indication of the feelings, wishes and fears of the villagers. For example, the following appeared: "Frank used to be here." "God kill the Minotaur." "Let us live in peace." "No more of this." "Help us!"

A picture of a large red demon bore the caption "King Minos." Another symbol was a minotaur drawn inside a circle with a solid bar across it indicating "forbidden."

The teacher, in role, entered the area close to the wall and began to examine the symbols and messages. In the scene that followed, the teacher, working in role, introduced herself as the parent of an Athenian youth destined to be sacrificed to the Minotaur. She wanted to know if there was anything that might be done to prevent the tragedy. At first the children, quickly slipping into the roles of villagers, wanted to know how someone from Athens had come ashore and wanted to determine if she were actually a traitor. Once satisfied that they could trust the stranger, they quickly referred to the events of the story to explain the present situation, then confided their own thoughts about the annual ritual. "When the Athenian youths are led from the ships to the Labyrinth I feel ashamed," said one villager. "Each spring my family and I hide in a cave when the Athenian boys and girls are brought to the Minotaur," said another. The stranger then challenged the villagers to accompany her to the palace of King Minos and let their true feelings be known. The villagers protested vigorously that such action would be futile, and would result in the deaths of all involved. The teacher, still in role, rebuked the villagers, accusing them of being little more than animals, hiding in caves and living in misery. The villagers were stunned at this accusation, but no one ventured forth to accompany the stranger, who said, "I go now to appeal to King Minos not only for the life of my own daughter, but for your lives too." The drama ended.

Although the nature of this kind of work will be discussed later, it is important to draw attention to several of its positive outcomes. Children who had expressed little enthusiasm for the story initially became quite vocal during the activity. Children who might be characterized as weaker readers participated as fully as the others, arguing vociferously when occasion demanded it. All the children became problem posers and joined in the spirit of inquiry with considerable commitment. All the children had time to savour the story, formulate their responses to it and make their meanings public.

Designing a Response Repertoire

Mouse goes everywhere. Through rich men's houses she creeps, visiting even the poorest. At night, with her little bright eyes, she watches the doing of secret things and no treasure chamber is so safe but she can tunnel through and see what is hidden there.

In the old days she wove four story children from all that she saw, and to each of these she gave a gown of different colours — white, red, blue and black. The stories became her children and lived in her house and served her, because she had no children of her own.

North American Indian folktale

In this book, we are most concerned with working with the whole class as a community. Safeguards lie in seeking the many modes of responding as a repertoire of choices, and in letting the children select and direct their own learning as much as possible. We may begin with a concept — set out art supplies, divide the class into discussion groups, organize an interview — but the children will direct the meaning making, and we as teachers will have to be sensitive to their wants and needs. Because we story together, the group of young people will have to cooperate and collaborate in carrying out activities. Not all children will be working on identical projects: some may be in groups, others may be partners, and others may work on their own for the moment. Nonetheless — in order to refocus, to share, to demonstrate — the children will come together and learn from each other in the community setting.

The Girl Who Loved the Wind

Children want a good yarn. They want to be drawn into stories, to be part of them, and at times to identify with them. For example, after listening to Jane Yolen's *The Girl Who Loved the Wind*, one class expressed considerable interest in the servants in the story. Since the servants scarcely figured in the tale, the teacher was puzzled by this response. The children explained that the merchant in the story (the girl's father) was a mean-tempered man. He had lost his daughter to the wind and as far as they were concerned, the servants would bear the brunt of his anger and frustration. The teacher had built a lesson around predicting how the girl would manage in her new life, living with the wind. The children weren't interested. As far as they were concerned, she had escaped living like a virtual prisoner in her father's house and had a new life. It was the fate of those left behind they were concerned about. The teacher quickly picked up on this and the result was a stimulating story adventure. What this illustrates is the need for teachers to take the time to help their students pursue responses. Too often, teachers feel pressed to offer a quick solution or invoke closure. Sometimes, it is as important to pursue the playful and spontaneous as it is to adhere to the teacher-initiated, "serious" direction.

Some types of stories dictate the work that will follow: controversial endings require talk for clarification; a beautifully illustrated picture book may beg for art or media activities. Similarly, some groups of children will be hesitant to share unless a sense of trust is created; the room in which the children experience the story may necessitate specific types of work. We hope that as we demonstrate particular lessons in which children respond to a story, teachers will use professional judgment in determining their own response program. Our advice would be to listen to the children, listen to the story and listen to your own teaching wisdom.

Central to our own work with young people has been the idea of "lengthening the period of incubation." For many children, a single reading of a story is followed by the answering of questions (often written) which tend to stress surface responses. We need to draw on the children's existing oral and literary backgrounds. What might happen if we were to provide for several readings of the story, develop multi-sensory activities to enhance interpretive work, and make children aware of themselves as makers and co-makers of story?

We like to encourage children to develop a sense of ownership about their reading; to become involved in words and worlds; to respond to a story in a variety of ways; to engage in a highly social and interactive way with story.

We have set out eight response modes in the repertoire that teachers can use, but we admit that each mode is not discrete from the others. Roleplaying will involve talk; writing may involve roleplay: the story we retell may be written down. However, we trust that teachers will make use of the components of response in innovative and exciting ways, and that they will develop their own methods of organizing storying activities.

What follows is a brief overview of the eight response modes; each will be discussed in greater detail later in the chapter.

Story Talk

- gossiping, reflecting and commenting about stories
- discussing our connections to the story, who we are in the story, the story events, the context, the impact
- talking about other story sets of which we are reminded, such as other genres, versions, themes, styles, authors, cultures, arts, structures
- having presentations, seminars, debates about the story issues
- discussing the authors and the people they have written about, background information that supports the authors
- brainstorming, problem-solving, making decisions about issues and problems depicted in the story
- establishing buzz groups and literature circles for discussions
- exploring feelings and thoughts both inside and outside the story
- generating questions and connections that arise from the story
- sharing discoveries about the story and ourselves

Telling and Retelling Stories

- relating our own anecdotes revealed by the story
- retelling the story from a personal point of view
- revisiting the story in role as a witness or character
- telling other stories that connect to or grow from this story
- playing storytelling games and activities growing out of the story
- revisiting the story in role as a witness or character in the story

Story Drama

- roleplaying situations from the story
- developing analogies to the story that are constructed together into drama
- placing characters from the story in new contexts
- using the mood, setting or atmosphere of the story as the basis for building drama
- exploring the story through movement, mime or puppetry

Reading Aloud

- sharing favourite sections aloud with friends
- reading selected pieces from other sources that connect to the book
- reading our own written responses to others
- introducing the story to others by reading a section aloud
- taping the story for a listening centre
- building a cooperative chant for choral speaking by reading some of the dialogue as script
- reading the narration aloud while others move or mime
- reading to a buddy or a younger child
- using the story as a source for scripts, as in readers' theatre

Writing Our Own Stories

- patterning our own stories from the original
- writing versions and variants of the story
- writing in role as characters involved with the story
- connecting information and research to the story
- developing plot diagrams and story webs

- inventing other stories inspired by this one
- writing letters to authors, characters, each other
- using journals to record thoughts and emotions elicited by the story

Parallel Reading

- reading other stories by the same author or illustrator
- reading other stories connected to the theme, concept, style or culture of the original
- locating background information and research by reading about the author or illustrator
- reading non-fiction stories that relate to the story
- finding reviews and reports about the book, the time, the setting or the author
- reading related stories written by other children

Story Art

- responding to ideas and feelings generated by the story through visual art
- setting up displays (for instance on bulletin boards), related to the story, theme or author
- mapping and graphing incidents in the story
- constructing three-dimensional art as a response to the story
- making posters, book covers, advertisements from the story
- using other media to represent the story — filmstrip, video, slides, films, videos or art reproductions relating to the story

Celebrating Stories and Authors

- interviewing guest authors and illustrators who visit
- creating book talks on a theme or concept the author explores
- attending a young authors' conference
- reading about authors, their views and lives
- writing and "publishing" our own books
- setting up special story celebrations for the whole school

Story Talk

How can we tune in to the children's thinking? Talking about the story is the most obvious way, but it is also one that has been much abused. Too often, what passes for talk about a story is merely a question-and-answer exercise which does little to expand the children's ability to respond.

In our work, story talk is the main ingredient of learning. The children talk to learn, storying in their own words, digging inside the narrative, floating above it, looking at it through magnifying glasses as they would a rare stamp, but most important revising and remaking their stories because of what others are thinking and revealing about their own stories.

Talking as a Community

Story talk with the whole class is an effective use of the talk mode, but it presents some difficulties. The number of children who can respond during the session is limited by time, opportunity, the ability of each child to speak aloud in large groups, and the group's ability to listen and respond sensitively and meaningfully. It may be difficult to hear unless the furniture is rearranged. Whole-class story talk may be best used for:

- brainstorming ideas about concerns for discussion in small groups;
- predicting and anticipating and clarifying the story to be read or heard; relating the story to other classroom concerns, such as thematic units, genre or style;
- building background about the story's setting, characters, concept structure;
- allowing a forum for summarizing, bringing forth points of view; sharing talk that happened during group interaction; allowing for feedback and different interpretations;
- giving opportunities for film and video versions of the story, and for authors and illustrators to lecture and demonstrate;
- setting up occasions for panels, seminars, public speakers, interviews, debates.

Story talk with the whole class presents a public forum for shared common experiences related to story. It allows for reflective talk after other response modes have been explored. Children can talk about the pictorial representations, the writing, the drama, the research, etc. The talk may focus on the story meanings or on the storyteller, on the children's identification with the story, on the stories within the story, on the background information, on the conflict, the resolution, the use of language, the difficulty of idiom, the word choice, the sentence structure, the style. It is important that the story talk at times be focused on the story itself, whether at the beginning of story talk, or as a summary or reflection of the dialogue that has taken place. The children may leave the story in order to understand it better, but they should return to see its reflection in the new learning, the new meaning that has grown from the talk.

Teachers often ask us where the ideas for story talk come from, but we have no single answer: the children, you, your parents, the street outside, the picture on the cover of a book, the name of the author, the colour of the jacket, the memories that flood from the story, the people like you in the story or those totally different, the tears of the boy in the back row, the laughter of the girl in the front, the rhythm of the words, the taste of them as you speak them, the newspaper at breakfast, the label on your shirt, the vibrations of the class, the rainbow in the sky. We tune in to the story with the children and together we make meaning through story talk.

To encourage story talk, the teacher often asks questions. The art of teaching lies in those questions and in handling the responses they engender. If we list our questions, we should be influenced by the children's questions as well, and therefore our personal list must never be seen as sequential or controlling or a dull agenda to be covered. They are signposts for the journey, and may be welcomed as directions when the talk becomes disjointed or argumentative.

Perhaps the most useful opening is, "Tell me about the story." This can begin the journey inside. The teacher must create a middle ground that allows the children to learn about the story, balancing the response among their experiences of it — thoughts, feelings and observations during and after the story — with the content of the story itself — theme, plot, characters and form.

In *Booktalk*, Aidan Chambers states that the art of reading lies in talking about what you have read. Like all readers, children want to discuss what they have enjoyed about a story, they want to explore those aspects of the story implicit in the text and ponder the connections they have made between the story and their own lives and the lives lived in other stories. He has provided a very useful chapter dealing with sample questions of an open-ended nature which have helped to provide lively interchanges of personal meanings among youngsters. Although a long list of sample questions has been provided, Chambers once stated in a workshop that the following four questions would stimulate all the discussion you could hope to have.

1. What parts did you like most?
2. What parts didn't you like?
3. Was there anything that puzzled you?
4. Did you notice anything in the story or poem that made a pattern?

Dinosaur Talk

A librarian had just completed a unit on dinosaurs, and the children from Kindergarten to Grade 6 had gathered in the library to celebrate the unit. We were asked to speak to them and share in the completion of their work, and we brought with us seven or eight books related to dinosaurs. However, the children had experienced all the books but one, *What Happened to Patrick's Dinosaurs?* by Carol Carrick, with pictures by Donald Carrick, a sequel to *Patrick's Dinosaurs*, which they knew. We read the book aloud and presented the illustrations to the audience. Once again, Patrick, defending his love of dinosaurs to his big brother Hank, describes how the dinosaurs were friendly to people, building them a modern world, until the unhappy dinosaurs left the earth and civilization took a backward step. When we, tongue-in-cheek, agreed with Patrick's theory, the children reacted strongly with all kinds of arguments and theories as to why dinosaurs and humans had not co-existed. Their information was surprising, and it was articulated well. Only the five-year-olds remained on our side in the discussion. At the end of the period, we were in disgrace with a victorious audience, until we brought out our last book, a rallying cry called *We're Back!*

Story Circles

Story talk in a small group offers a powerful dynamic for learning. The discussion can be spontaneous or directed. The children can put forward their own concerns or work from a stimulus-response sheet. They can meet together before reading to predict, anticipate and set the stage for the narrative. They can use story talk as the starting point for story projects of all kinds — researching, roleplaying, writing, storytelling, reading aloud, painting. The teacher may work with one group at a time, as moderator or contributor, or a student reader may volunteer or be selected. Some talk can be tape-recorded for playback as clarification or for another group to hear.

Story circles, like adult book circles, allow children to engage in booktalk. A typical story circle comprises three to five children who have chosen to read the same book from a collection offered by the teacher and who gather together to read, discuss and share responses. The purpose of the circle is to promote reading and encourage response to literature through discussions, and to provide opportunities for children to work in small groups that are usually child-centred. Children read the text silently — material is read aloud only to clarify a particularly confusing point, to support a point made in the discussion group or to celebrate the author.

At first, you will need to help children form groups and choose the books to be read. In addition, you will need to be a member of each group at some time, helping children to stay on task and explore the book in a meaningful way. It is important, when participating in discussions, to refrain from asking directed questions. Questions, particularly those that require short answers, can direct the route of a conversation, and make the person who asks them the centre of attention. Statements, on the other hand, extend the conversation and retain the group's equilibrium. Consider the implication of the question "What did you notice about..." with the statement "The author made me think about..." In this way, you can have the children consider a point without adding the stress of answering the question correctly. By participating in a discussion in such a way, children absorb techniques that extend discussions and allow group members to contribute freely. Children will soon be able to conduct an effective story circle without your participation.

This shift in interaction can be uncomfortable, at least initially, for both children and teachers. Discussions may be superficial — children will need time to practise conversation skills and explore facets of their reading that will lead to good discussions. Some children, particularly those who are shy, may have difficulty contributing to a discussion in which the standard rules of the classroom have changed. In these cases, you can encourage them to tell you or another member their thoughts. In turn, you can share them with the group. As well, the children can make their contribution to the group by reading from their journal or having a friend read their words. Encourage an environment where these children feel safe and where they can gradually begin to contribute to the group.

The transition will not be seamless and there may be a proliferation of silences that are abnormal in the typical classroom environment. Initially, you and the children will be more comfortable with a question-response environment in which you are viewed as the expert. Although it may be difficult, try to refrain from filling in when the conversation dwindles. Usually, it will begin again, but if it stretches on you can remind the children that this is their conversation and encourage them to take the lead.

After reading the story *Cloudland* by John Burningham, a group of Grade 2 children in Larry Swartz's classroom met in a story circle to share their responses to the book. *Cloudland* is the story of a boy named Albert who fell off a cliff and ended up in Cloudland, where he enjoyed playing with other cloud children. During the conversation, the children gave their opinions of the story (e.g., "I like the way the Queen was done and the clothing she wore"/"I like the expressions in the story like when he said 'he had his head in the clouds'"); expressed some puzzles they had ("I wonder why at the end the mother didn't say, 'We're so happy to see you!'"/"Why didn't they call a helicopter?") and commented on events from the story that most impressed them ("I like the way he was talking to himself using words like a baby"). Much talk focused on Burningham's illustrations, which are photographs of the sky combined with line drawings. Some children made connections to their own lives.

The following transcript is an excerpt of a conversation in which Matula, AJ, Nathan, Kate and Stephanie begin to consider what it would be like to be on Cloudland as well as to hypothesize how the cloud children came to live there:

Nathan: What if everybody in the clouds were invisible and nobody on the ground could see them? . . .only people in the clouds could see each other.

Kate: I'd like to be in Cloudland because you could float up in the air.

AJ: I would like to be there because you could be light as a feather. I think that would be really cool. I would only stay if my family was there. I would like to go to heaven or something. . .to see my animals who died. . .

Kate: I think I would like to go there because I want to really feel what the clouds feel like.

Nathan: I want to go there if only the good kids are there.

Matula: How do you know if they're good kids?

Nathan: If they were bad kids they would throw things off the clouds.

Stephanie: The queen said, "Nobody's ever left Cloudland before". . .Because everybody loves it. If I was going to be in Cloudland, I would only stay for half an hour.

AJ: I wonder if animals could go there.

Matula: Why didn't the other children leave like Albert did?

AJ:	Maybe their families passed away or something. . .or maybe the kids were walking up the mountain and they slipped and fell like Albert did. . .Maybe they were happy because there were more kids to play with on Cloudland and the Queen was like a mother to them.
Kate:	Maybe they are children who already died.
AJ:	Maybe Cloudland is their first stage and then they go up higher.
Kate:	Maybe they died in a car crash and they were all sisters and they came up in the clouds together. . .and then they stayed because they thought it was really cool and they didn't want to go back.
AJ:	Albert was there because he fell. He was brave and he didn't scream "Help! Help!". If he didn't fall on the clouds he would have died.
Matula:	I feel sorry for Albert. I bet his mother and father were worried.
Nathan:	Maybe the other kids in Cloudland didn't like their parents. . .The two kids went up the mountain and then two other kids came along and they didn't like their parents because they were mean. All four of them fell off the mountain and fell on the clouds.
Matula:	And they were happy. I wonder if Albert would be happy if he stayed.
Nathan:	If Albert didn't go home, he would be dead like the other children on their way to Heaven.
AJ:	If Albert didn't go home, his family would die of a broken heart.

Ten Ways to Promote Booktalk
By Larry Swartz

1. Choose good books.

If a story helps me think of stories from my own life, then I am encouraged to share it with children with the hope that it will resonate for them too. Several books which I find help me with the job of having the children share their own stories are: *The Relatives Came* by Cynthia Rylant, *Night Noises* by Mem Fox, *When I Was Nine* by James Stevenson, *The Dust Bowl* by David Booth, *The Auction* by Jan Andrews and *Owl Moon* by Jane Yolen.

2. Take the time to listen.

Just as a ritual time needs to be set aside for reading stories to the class, a deliberate time needs to be established for story discussion. From time to time a structured event needs to be introduced to have the children share stories they have been reminded of as they listened to the story.

However, I find that more often than not, children are sparked to tell stories spontaneously without a prompt from the teacher. These stories cannot be ignored, as they are opportunities that make our curriculum truly authentic.

3. Allow digression.

The stories that children tell may not necessarily be connected to the topic at hand. Digressions will emerge, especially if a longer period of time is given for conversation. We could ask: "What made you think of that story?" Often a word or a snippet of narrative will bring stories of the children's own lives to the surface. Recently when I went to visit a Kindergarten class, I told them that I had a new book about a cat. One child put up his hand and told me that his uncle took him to the zoo, and he told about the polar bears he saw. Another child then told us about her visit to the zoo.

4. Tell your own stories.

If the best response to a story is to tell a story, we teachers can tell stories from our own lives that have come to mind as we read a book. By sharing our own stories, we are not only modeling what we hope the children will do, but we are demonstrating how one makes personal connections and gains personal meaning from reading. Sometimes it is important to make this connection very explicit. When a sentence or passage I read stirs up a memory, I draw the children's attention to it and tell the children, "This reminds me of the time that I…" When I was reading *The Relatives Came* by Cynthia Rylant aloud to the children, I told them about a family reunion when I was five years old and my cousins from Florida came to visit. When I told the story about falling out the window while fooling around, the children had many, many stories to share about accidents in their lives.

5. Organize small groups.

It is important to introduce a variety of groupings (pairs and small groups, gender-balanced, organized by the teacher or freely chosen by the children). A colleague of mine, Brian Crawford, introduces story talk very successfully with his Kindergarten class. When Brian finishes reading a story he tells the children to find a partner. Each child in turn is given time to tell what he or she thought about the book and what they thought about as they listened to the book.

6. Initiate response before, during or after reading a story.

Sometimes when I introduce a story, I ask the children to talk about what the title of the book reminds them of. For instance, *Canoe Days* by Gary Paulsen was recently chosen as the daily read-aloud and many children had stories to share about being on a canoeing, camping or boat trip. As I continue to read a story I usually find that one or two children put up their hands to tell us what they have thought of. Sometimes during the reading of a story, I take the opportunity to pause and ask the children if they ever had an experience like the one described in the book. Other times when I finish a story, I organize small groups in which students are given the opportunity to talk about their responses with their peers. After the small group discussion, we make these conversations public in a whole class context.

7. Honour a variety of connections.

When I introduced *The Rabbit* by John Burningham to a group of Grade 1 children, I asked if anyone had any experiences with rabbits. I recognize that a large number of children in the class may never have seen or touched a rabbit. Limiting the talk to things that happened to them personally may not include the majority. To stretch the realm of their connections, children need to be encouraged to think of others they know who might have had similar experiences to the ones being discussed. Broadening connections can release more stories to be told.

8. Ask questions.

Not only should the teacher be asking questions, but opportunities should be offered to classmates to ask questions of the storyteller. When significant questions are asked, the storyteller can better shape the story as he or she conveys specific details connected to it. Besides making the story more evocative, questions might lead a child into further inspecting his or her memory and uncovering its significance.

9. Invite children to write their stories.

Sometimes children need encouragement to move from the story into written narratives. The experiences they write about have a formative effect on the child's developing narrative voice and through this his developing sense of self. In *Living Between the Lines*, Lucy Calkins tells us that "when we write memoir, we must discover not only the moments of our lives but the meanings in those moments." Children have enough memories and enough stories to tell, but the challenge, according to Calkins, is to find out how particular moments fit into the plot lines of our lives.

10. Do nothing.

When children listen to a book, stories may wander through their heads but these stories may not be released and made public. It is not always necessary to have the children share their story responses. Just let the story be. Sometimes, the stories that have been awakened need to remain private in the minds of children. Although in our classrooms we may want the children to release these stories to enrich the community of storytellers and conversationalists, we need to be respectful of the silence of some.

Telling and Retelling Stories

Telling Life Tales

A child's identity, culture and origins will be revealed in each story told, and the resulting experience will give the original tale a pattern and texture that will enrich both the teller and the told. We need to revel in the identification and personalizing that a child has made with a story. Each retelling may incorporate a new dialect, different syntax, unique rhythms, particular observations, emotional shadings, specific locales and alternative time frames. The story fabric becomes elaborately embroidered as each child weaves a personal retelling.

We can strengthen the children's story lives by making the classroom a safe place and a staring point for sharing life tales:

- encouraging spontaneous personal storytelling on each occasion when it is appropriate;
- asking children to connect their own experiences to what they have read about or listened to;
- using special events (a touring play, a professional storyteller, a visiting guest) as an occasion for sharing memories stimulated by the experience;
- allowing time for children to recount life stories formally during current events, or informally on rainy day recesses, or at clean-up times;
- using polished life tales as building blocks for personal writing, for painting or inside the safety of roleplaying in a drama lesson;
- helping children to use real-life stories as the basis for their fiction creations, both strengthening the believability of their writing and offering them a means for handling issues too sensitive to be told in a straightforward manner;
- designing opportunities for deep listening on a visit to a home for senior citizens, or a hospice;
- arranging for sharing stories with a buddy class of different-aged children in the school, or having a local high school class come and tell polished life tales about their years in elementary grades;
- sharing stories for each and every celebration involving different members of the class;
- family stories (with permission) to be retold for parents' night;
- bravely telling your own life tales from both your professional life and your personal life to strengthen or model a point that arises during a discussion or a shared reading. Swapping tales is still the best way of motivating your students to tell their stories.

The stories which our students tell about themselves should be honoured in our classrooms, for it is through their stories that they build their self-esteem and sense of belonging in the world, and of course, how they come to understand how stories work.

In *Language Matters*, Alan Newland, a British educator, describes his storying experiences with a group of children in his school:

The Patchwork Quilt by Valerie Flournoy is a book about connecting the scraps of one's shared existence into a significant whole. A little girl, housebound by a cold, watches her granny put together a quilt from the scraps of her family's old clothing. But the granny falls seriously ill, and the task of finishing the quilt is taken up at first by the little girl and then by her mother. The quilt's completion becomes an act of faith in their grandmother's recovery, and her recovery in turn a powerful assertion of women's arts and crafts, of the 'old' values that the granny was so frightened had been lost by her daughter's generation, and of the significance of their shared experience as a family. I asked the children in my class of third year junior to bring in treasured possessions from their earliest memories; old clothes, favourite toys, family photographs. We sat in a circle and talked about them. We giggled at each other's teddy bears, sailing boats, old snap-shots and listened to the stories behind them. One story led to another, and although they were all different, like the quilt in the story, we began connecting our patches with a common thread. Once a week we spent the whole morning doing this and the children not only became engrossed in each other's life stories, but they listened, reflected and told new ones with a rapidly developing competence.

Their concern for each other was obvious. Interruptions were few and confined to making connections of common interests. We would alternate between talking in twos and threes and gathering together to share as a class. As the first few weeks passed with the children bringing in more and more photos, old toys, watches, musical instruments, heirlooms and treasured possessions of every kind, it became apparent that a peculiar kind of sharing was going on.

One week a girl brought in a piece of dress material worn by her mother as a maternity smock, accompanied by a letter written by mum recalling the days spent wearing it. A broken old watch was given to one child's mother as a final parting gift of a dying grandfather. The powerful and important memories evoked by attachment to such treasured objects is not difficult to comprehend, but what was more elusive to my understanding and what seemed more interesting was the re-assessing and reshaping of experience that seemed to be going on. Changes in the way they were comprehending experience seemed to be taking place and then an incident of particular significance took place which helped me sort all this out a bit more clearly.

Two years ago my mother died and I began wearing her wedding ring. This was noticed by my class at the time and so I explained it to them. In one of our morning 'tellingstory' sessions a child related an incident of finding some valuable jewelry and taking it, with her mother, to the police.

"I wouldn't do that," said Nicola, only half jokingly. "Would you?" I asked.

"Yes" she replied, "finders keepers, innit? Or sell it, you could take it down the jewelry shop and sell it." Some others agreed, especially if you could sell it. Then someone reminded us all that "you wouldn't like it if it was your jewelry that was lost though, would you?" Here I saw my chance to intervene. I took off my mother's ring and held it out to Nicola. Her eyes were fixed on it and she was understandably apprehensive. She knew what I was going to ask.

"What would you do if you found this one Nic? Would you sell it?" She didn't answer, but smiled back at me nervously. "Go on, hold it," I said trying to reassure her, but her friend Tanya, sitting next to her, came to her aid. "No you can't sell that," she said quietly, "it's part of your mum." Everyone was quiet, though not embarrassed. "But how do we know that that lost jewelry wasn't just as important to the person who lost it as this ring is to me?" I asked. At that moment, I could almost see the stories swirling about their heads as to why that jewelry might be important to someone. So I asked them; "Why do you think that jewelry was important to the person who lost it?" Some of the stories that followed were short and simple, others were elaborate and beautiful. "Everything's important to someone, sometime, isn't it?" said Natalie, a nine-year-old. I sat looking at her, thinking what an incredible insight that was for a mind so young, but it was also an observation which, on reflection, seemed to show an enormous grasp of the limitless possibilities of narrative.

Telling the Stories of Others

Retelling a story in your own words is one of the most effective ways to achieve a reflective response. Fortunately, this is an activity that can be organized simply.

So often reading and the activities around reading are "hurry up, hurry up" — we are getting through the text, the story, the book, the course, whatever. You miss so much if you don't have a chance to linger with a story. But by encouraging children to retell a story, you can enable them to go back to that story and find out more and more. One of the things we like to do with children is round robin storytelling (not to be confused with round robin reading, which is now taboo). One after the other, in a circle, we simply retell a story we have all heard or read, in our own words, with the idea that it is the responsibility of the whole group to tell the story. Each of us only has a part of it for a few seconds before we pass it on. Using that as a device we have been able to get children thinking about point of view, and telling stories in the first person, third person, or mixing up a first-person narration with a third-person narration, two first-person speakers, and all of these in combination. Together they produce interesting storytelling, and the more we do it, the more the children begin to project themselves imaginatively into the text.

As the story is told, we begin to see a very rich new story appearing. In the context of that new story, we will very often ask the children their feelings and thoughts about the characters. We then come out of the circle and do interviews with each other. "Let's interview this person. Pretend you are a reporter. What would you like to ask? What would you like to know?" That simple technique gets the children talking about the characters. Next, we might have the whole bunch altogether, all telling stories at once, or we might have a surprise interview with a character, with only three questions, just like the three wishes so common in folktales. Then we get them to refine their understanding of what they think is important about the story, arguing and struggling with the three questions that are going to give them the inside information. After that we go back into our storytelling circles and tell the story one more time, only now we must reveal a big secret that we discovered about the story that nobody else knows.

We have sometimes recorded these little story circles and listened to the tapes. Often what started out as a very narrow, tiny little segment of a story has grown and become very rich. We go back and examine other questions. How did the author tell this story? How did we tell this story? At this point we are so inside the story we're getting into everything from character development to dialogue to structure, without ever using any of those words. The storytelling way offers hands-on experience.

Spontaneous retelling in a story circle is one of the most effective ways in which children can reveal what a story they have just heard has meant to them. With such retelling, no one has the burden of the entire story. As the story travels around the circle, each participant can add as much or as little as desired. Indeed, some children often prefer to pass on the initial round or so until they begin to get more involved in the story. The beauty of this activity is its simplicity and the opportunity it affords each child to put the story into his or her own words and to make explicit personal story imagery. It is also an extremely effective way to hone listening skills. The same kind of story retelling also works effectively in pairs.

In this instance, the story alternates back and forth, perhaps at a signal by the teacher. Initially, it helps to keep signaling a change every twenty to thirty seconds until the children feel confident that they can make more extended runs. Small groups can function in like fashion once the children have become accustomed to working with stories this way. Sometimes it's good to have members of a group act out a story as one of its members tells it. Again, the emphasis is on spontaneous retelling. Once under way, the listeners add actions, sound effects, choruses, whatever comes into their heads. Such activity often frees up the responses to a story and makes the children more aware of the possibilities that exist for retelling that story.

Communal Storytelling

Another form of large-group, spontaneous retelling might be called communal composition. It involves composing orally together from a subject or theme. In some ways, it resembles rapping. The object of the activity is to improvise with words, rhythms and sounds using a single theme or subject.

The theme or subject is discussed in terms of what information the group has about it. This material is sorted, classified and ordered into an "out-loud" experience. For example, a composition on how words play might result in an inventory of all the ways this occurs (e.g., palindromes, puns, etc.) and examples of these in action. A framework of unison choruses, antiphonal choruses, solos and songs is then developed.

One teacher capitalized on her classes' interest in proverbs. She introduced to her children John Agard's *Say It Again, Granny*, a collection of twenty poems based on Caribbean proverbs. It became the source for the following group composition.

All:	Granny says (chanted three times with sharp rythmic clapping "dada-da-dada" interspersed between the words).
Group A (unison):	Early to bed and early to rise Makes one healthy, wealthy, and wise.
Group B (unison):	That's what Granny says!
Group B (unison):	Birds of a feather flock together.
Group A (unison):	That's what Granny says!
Group B (unison):	Mother, may I go out to swim?
Group B (unison):	Yes, darling granddaughter. Hang your clothes on a hickory stick But don't go near the water.
Group B (unison chanting under solos):	Granny always telling you
Solo A:	A stitch in time saves nine,
Solo B:	Don't count your chickens before they hatch,
Solo C:	Still waters run deep.

The end of the piece was played as a game. The children were divided into groups and given a proverb to disguise by "padding" it. For example, the proverb "A watched pot never boils" might become "A vessel containing H20 seldom reaches 100°C when scrutinized constantly." Each group in turn chanted its "padded proverb" while the rest of the class tried to echo the original one.

While much of the preceding may not seem to be storytelling, it is important to point out that language creativity or word play reinforces the fact that words have sounds, rhythms, spellings and visual shapes — all qualities that can be played with and that contribute to the power of language which makes a story live. Prepared retellings differ from the spontaneous mainly in that the children work from print sources rather than spoken ones. The emphasis is still on having them use their own words, which can be tricky because where print is involved, the children often think that everything that is written down must be reproduced exactly.

Working from print sources can involve techniques such as the following:

1. The entire class is divided into groups of no more than three members.
2. Each group is given a piece of a story to retell as a trio. How the group retells it is entirely up to them; the only rule is that each member of the group must be involved in telling.
3. The groups reconvene and form a story circle. The group with the opening segment begins. The remaining groups have to figure out where their segment fits and come in at the appropriate time.

Finding the Stories Within

Among the most challenging material to deal with is that which might be described as elliptical. As 'the told,' we are given only bits and pieces to work with, but must work with them to try and construct the whole story. In order to get anywhere with this kind of material, lots of inference must be encouraged. "Micky Thumps" is a good example of a selection that demands a great deal of the reader's thought and imagination in order to find the stories within.

Micky Thumps

As I was going down Treak Street
For half a pound of treacle,
Who should I meet but my old friend Micky Thumps?
He said to me, "Wilt thou come to our wake?
I thought a bit,
I thought a bit,
I said I didn't mind:
So I went.

As I was sitting on our doorstep
Who should come by but my old friend Micky Thumps' Brother?
He said to me, "Wilt thou come to our house?
Micky is ill."
I thought a bit,
I thought a bit,
I said I didn't mind:
So I went.

And he were ill.
He were gravely ill.
He said to me,
"Wilt thou come to my funeral, mon, if I die?"
I thought a bit,
I thought a bit,
I said I didn't mind:
So I went.

And it were a funeral.
Some stamped on his grave:
Some spat on his grave:
But I scraped my eyes out for my old friend Micky Thumps.

Anonymous

In one Grade 6 class, after a brief discussion of friendship and what the students considered important qualifiers and responsibilities associated with it, the teacher arranged the students in groups of four and asked them to read the poem silently, then out loud together, helping each other with vocabulary and rhythms.

The teacher explained that the poem was like a bicycle wheel missing the outer rim and several spokes. "Our task will be to try to rebuild the wheel."

Each group was asked to choose a recorder and then "take a mental walk" through the poem, pausing to notice what caught their eye. The recorders were given large sheets of newsprint and instructed to make three columns labeled "What we know," "What we think we know," and "What puzzles us."

Following is an example of what one group of students recorded about the selection.

What we know	What we think we know	What puzzles us
Micky has a brother	Micky was not well-liked	Why didn't people like him?
Micky got sick	Micky died	What is treacle?
The speaker is Micky's friend	We think the poem is from Jamaica	What is he ill with?
Micky has enemies	We think Micky knows he is going to die	Where does the story take place?
Micky lived with his mother		Is this Micky's real name?

Recorders all read their jottings to the class, who were encouraged to add anything they liked to their lists. The object of this was to ensure that all the students had information to consider.

The teacher asked all the students to pretend that they were distant relatives of Micky's and that each of them had had passed on to them something that belonged to Micky. Each student in turn told members of their group what they had (these ranged from family rings to musical instruments, letters, diaries, items of clothing and even body parts…a glass eye, a wooden leg).

With this simple activity, a profile of Micky began to emerge. Now the teacher asked each group to create a tableau on one of the following:

- Micky as his mother would like him to be remembered;
- Micky as his second grade teacher remembers him;
- Micky as his brother would like him to be remembered;
- Micky as his fifth grade teacher remembers him;
- Micky as the poem's narrator remembers him;
- Micky as his eighth grade teacher remembers him.

The teacher arranged the tableaux in a circle and one after the other they were displayed and viewed.

The class then discussed what they thought they knew about Micky's life. The teacher called for volunteers to take the roles of:

- Micky's brother;
- Micky's mother;
- the narrator;
- Micky's second grade teacher.

Each of these players took up a position in one corner of the room.

The teacher assigned the roles of news reporters to the remaining members of the class. They were to interview one of the four subjects and report back to their editor (the teacher in role).

Students were given five minutes to conduct their interviews. They all reported back to the teacher, who interviewed them about the information they had gathered.

The four subjects who had been interviewed stood outside the group. They were permitted to challenge anything reported which they considered erroneous. The reporters would only listen to the rebuttals; they would not engage with the speakers.

At the end of the meeting, the teacher, still in role, asked the students to prepare their stories and to supply an eye-catching headline.

Later the students reconvened to share their stories and discuss their interviews about Micky Thumps.

By bringing together all the stories in the piece, stimulated by images or words, and comparing them, children began to see the big picture. The aim of the work was to encourage inquiry on the part of the children rather than to re-create the story. Roleplaying was employed in several situations because it is such an effective way to encourage children to step into the events of books and into the lives of characters. The imaginations of the children were stretched by encouraging them to explore incidents briefly hinted at and incidents that didn't occur but might have, and to comment on story events in the shoes of characters who were or were not present.

In so doing, the children's understanding of the themes, events and characters was amplified, and their experiences of the story broadened.

Telling a Family of Stories

Storytelling of this nature can also provide opportunities to visit "story families" in ways that familiarize children with important collections that they might not otherwise discover. For example, the "Jataka Tales," though little known in America, have been told for over two thousand years in other parts of the world. Attributed to Buddha, they are to eastern cultures what Aesop's fables are to the west. The stories feature animals that speak. They are, in fact, a wonderful introduction to other animal stories of enchantment which children might encounter, such as *The Jungle Book* (Rudyard Kipling), *Charlotte's Web* (E. B. White), *Abel's Island* (William Steig), *The Sheep Pig* (Dick King Smith), *Watership Down* (Richard Adams) and *Ratha's Creature* (Clare Bell). This is also an interesting way to explore genres. The "tall tale" or "trickster tale" could become the focus of work, which, if approached imaginatively, could span the globe, inviting wonderful comparisons. Think of *Doctor Coyote* by John Bierhorst, where Aesop's fables were carried to South America, taken over by the Inca and incorporated into their Coyote Trickster Stories. Prepared retellings can also involve completely changing the form of a story.

Building a Tower of Language

One group of children used Leon Garfield's unique retelling of the story of the tower of Babel, *Nimrod's Tower*, as the source for their invention. They proceeded by isolating key moments in the story and rewriting them as playground songs, skipping rhymes and ball-bouncing chants.

Here are just a couple of the pieces they composed:

1. The Chant of the Foreman

    Stay at work! Stay at work! says foreman to workers
    Stay at work! Stay at work! says foreman to workers
    Stay at work! Stay at work! says foreman to workers
    You've got to build higher or we'll stop your pay
    Heave bricks and mortar, says foreman to workers (repeat twice)
    You must pass through clouds or we'll stop your pay.
    Higher and higher, says foreman to workers (repeat twice)
    You must reach for eagles or we'll stop your pay.

2. The Cry of the Spectators

    Old King Nimrod climbed his tower
    Old King Nimrod stayed an hour
    Old King Nimrod challenged the Lord
    Old King Nimrod was quickly floored.

Once they had assembled their pieces, the children formed groups and each group worked with one piece. The work involved speaking the words aloud and inventing a game that might accompany the words. Balls, ropes and hoops were available to be incorporated into the games.

When all the games were invented and the accompanying rhymes integrated with the action patterns, the children established a plan for retelling. They decided to create a busy playground scene alive with sound and movement. The story was played out in a gymnasium. The children cleared the space. Then, on the signal of a bell, they streamed into the playing area, set up their games and commenced the stories. On prearranged whistle signals, everyone froze action while each group, in agreed-upon order, did its part.

A ringing school bell ended the action and the children cleared the floor as in the beginning.

Neighbourhood Stories

Everyone has a neighbourhood story about the house you don't visit on Hallowe'en or the strange neighbour who strikes terror into your heart whenever your ball accidentally ends up on his or her lawn. Perhaps there is a special tree or a particular animal that is the subject of much neighbourhood chat. A mystery, a special happening, a tree downed in a storm, an annual bed race — every neighbourhood has stories.

One book that might stir some neighbourhood story making is *The Green Lion of Zion Street* by Julia Fields. In this lively narrative poem, a group of school children, bored with waiting for the school bus, embark on a foggy morning adventure across a high bridge to the spot where a stone lion prowls. As they approach it, they let their imaginations run wild and end up not only frightening themselves, but missing the bus as well. What child hasn't let a shadow, a statue, a gnarled tree, a lane way or a creaking door become the object of a wild fantasy?

Cynthia Rylant's book *When I Was Young in the Mountains* is so carefully told that listeners young and old are ready to share their own stories of porch swings, corner stores, grandma's kitchen, swimming with snakes in the water, baptisms where the candidate is immersed completely. When they hear "For I was in the mountains, and that was always enough," storyers conjure up their own special places from childhood and from today, placing their own personal narrative alongside those of Cynthia Rylant. A walk together around the school neighbourhood should furnish clues for dozens of local tales — a hole in the ground, a dark grotto, a cryptic message scribbled on a wall.

Having older children share stories with students in younger grades is a wonderful way to bring about critical understanding because it is always easier to discuss literature that you have outgrown, that belongs to your past — but work that is probably new to your audience, or just beyond their capacity as readers. All good critical discussion and writing come from familiarity with a story and from having grown beyond the experience of it.

Storytelling Activities

Storytelling activities can take many forms.

- Children can tell stories in a circle, with a partner in a frozen picture, chorally or as narration for mime. They can improvise from the story, change the story or find new stories to tell within the story.
- Storytelling can provide the initial starting point for drama work; it can reveal an unexplained idea in even a well-known story; it can focus particular details; it can be a review of what has already taken place, or it can be a way of building reflection in-role.
- Using picture books with little or no text, such as *Tuesday*, by David Weisner, children can describe in their own words what they see happening, sometimes supplying the characters with what they feel is appropriate dialogue. Showing children unusual and exciting pictures may also promote storytelling.
- Children may enjoy playing the different characters as they tell the story. Or children may dramatize a story while it is being told, assuming the parts of different characters (e.g., a witch, a bird, or two lost children).
- As the storyteller spins the tale, the teacher may signal for someone to continue the story, or another child may choose to continue on his or her own at a dramatic pause in the story.

- The children sit in a circle on the floor so that they can all see each other. A subject or style of story is identified. A story is built as each child in turn contributes one (or two, or three, or more) words. A child may begin a new sentence at any appropriate moment. A student may add as much as he or she wishes to the story. A "talking stick" is held by each child when it is his or her turn to speak, and is passed on to the next child when the speaker stops (sometimes in mid-phrase). The teacher may stop and start speakers at random.
- The teacher tells an improvised story, pauses every so often and points to someone in the group to add an appropriate word. "Once upon a time there was a young…" "He walked until suddenly…" "He said…"
- The teacher asks the children to imagine that they are about to start on a great adventure. The students decide individually where they are, who they are and why they are embarking on this adventure. It is midnight and they are standing outside a castle; or at the edge of an enchanted forest; or in front of a modern tower block; or outside a prison camp. They must enter this place to accomplish some vital deed. They may decide they are heroes, or spies, and must try to be aware of all the attributes that such characters are likely to possess. Their journeys will be beset with dangers and difficulties. Individually, the students move off on their various quests. When each quest has reached its moment of greatest tension, that child freezes.

  The students then choose partners and each tells the other the story of his or her adventure. In the telling, the stories usually become even more exciting and the difficulties exaggerated, as do the courage and resourcefulness of the teller. Pairs may combine to make groups and small groups to make larger groups, so that eventually some pupils will be talking to quite a large number of others.
- The students sit in a circle. The teacher chooses two narrators to share an original story between them. One tells a short portion of the story, stops to let the other person continue, then takes over again after a few minutes. The rest of the students become the characters and objects in the story, and act it out silently. Their participation may influence the shape of the story.

  This game can also be played with the narrators providing the story and the actors making up their own speeches.
- The teacher introduces the subject of storytelling "occasions," when people gather together to relate various stories. To give students practice in sustained narration, the teacher asks them to pretend that they are part of such an occasion — e.g., when Robin Hood and his band of outlaws recall their most famous escapades; or when the world's greatest spies and secret agents have their annual meeting to recount their greatest exploits; or when members of a tribe tell stories of the deeds of their ancestors and narrate the legends of the tribe. Once the teacher has established a situation, the participants discuss their roles and a storytelling session takes place.

- The children work in pairs. One child retells the story which the teacher has told; then the second child tells the story back to the first child.
- A short tall tale or "whopper" is an excellent vehicle for children to develop skill in recapitulating stories and also to gain practice in the role of storyteller.

"Two snakes had a fight. After circling for a while, one grabbed the other's tail and started swallowing it. Then the other grabbed the first snake's tail and started swallowing it. By the time they finished, they had swallowed each other."

Each child has a different story to tell. The children retell their stories in a circle, either as narrators or as first-person participants. As an interesting variant, the teacher asks the children to tell their stories in random order, but with each child attempting to introduce a narrative hook to link his or her story to the preceding one.

The Storytelling Club

In the elementary school where Judy Caulfield teaches, she runs a voluntary storytelling club for the children once a week. Her doctoral thesis grew out of this work:

It is 11:30. Lunch time. The Kindergarten room is full of students ranging from Grade 3 to Grade 6. They are a mixed group. The kindergarten furniture is a challenge. Students are crouched around small tables, gathered around the short, squat table in the cloakroom or clustered around the large wooden electrical spool with small chairs drawn up. There are over 30 of them. The air is filled with their talk. This isn't their assigned lunchroom. This disparate group is here because they have chosen to be here. Attendance is called over the hubbub with a voice barely heard. Twenty minutes later, the same group is packed together — sardined into the space covered by a small rug. Now they are silent. They are gathered around a teacher who is telling a story. All eyes are focused on her. As she speaks, the children make eye contact easily and comfortably. At times one of their heads will nod. They lean slightly forward — one moment smiling, the next moment opening their eyes wide with surprise or delight. Barely a whisper is heard from them. There is a chant in the middle of the story that will be repeated with variation throughout. The storyteller's voice swings with the chant. The next time she repeats it in the story some of the students begin to join in:

"Cow of mine, cow of mine,
Have you ever seen a maid of mine?
With a wig and a wag
And a long leather bag,
Stole all the money
I ever had!"

At first only one or two of the students quietly repeat the chant. But each time the chant reoccurs in the story more and more join in until finally they are all merrily chanting and wigwagging their bodies to the rhythm of the words. What's happening? The Storytelling Club! Once a week this group of students meets with two teachers to immerse themselves in stories — listening, discussing and telling stories. When I moved to this school, I discovered, to my delight, another teacher who also knew and loved storytelling and traditional stories. We wanted a place and time for children to hear stories told. Few of our children had had opportunities to hear storytelling. We wanted them to have a chance to soak up, to absorb the rhythms of narrative language. Our goal was to immerse them in stories, story talk and storytelling in a supportive environment. We were both drawn to the traditional folk and fairytales that have been told and honed across generations.

One of my students, Draco, expresses this feeling of community when he discusses the school cabaret that is held for the student storytellers and a few friends at the end of the year: "We're telling stories and we're telling the people what we like to associate with-storytelling! We [also] get to associate with a lot of different people." For Draco, "associate" is a key word. It indicates for him the power of being in a community with like goals. It also indicates an identity. He is declaring to people that he wants to be seen as being connected with stories.

Our students are continually teaching us about how they connect to stories and storytelling. When another student, Karen, told the story *Rainbow Crow*, students were surprised that she'd heard the story three years ago and hadn't reread it since. How had she remembered it and why? With a bit of prompting Karen explained that she often retold the story to herself: "My last name is Crowe and I like that story!" A story where crow shows the courage, persistence, and daring to bring fire for the other animals may provide a powerful talisman for Karen.

Story Drama

Making sense of a story demands that the students apply their own experiences to those in the story. We need to constantly help the children go back and forth between their own stories and their own responses, translating the experiences of the story into the context of their own lives. Drama allows the children's own subjective worlds to come into play, helping them understand the meanings of the story as they live through related and connected drama experiences. In story drama, students are required to create personal responses of their own to the story. They can become involved in roleplaying, decision-making, problem-solving, verbal interaction, mime, movement and group process.

The teacher can use the story to provide a beginning point for drama, and the story can assist the teacher in giving form to that drama. The story and its strength enable the teacher to dip into the richness of the contexts that the author has provided. Drama becomes a tool for the exploration of the ideas, relationships and language of the story. The children are not limited to the facts or words in the story, since the story per se is not the prime focus. It may indeed happen that the children's appreciation and understanding of the story deepens after drama. However, the teacher must be concerned primarily with the developmental aspects of drama that occur as the children elaborate, extend and invent.

Story provides the framework for building drama, enriching the quality of the dramatic experience and imparting an artistic awareness to the lives of those involved. As students begin to explore the subtext of the story, they move from an enactment of the literal information into an exploration of the concepts that lie under the plot skeleton. They begin to draw upon their own experiences and to see story incidents from the viewpoint of both self and others, entwined in a role in the drama happening at that very moment. Perhaps the children are engaged in creating a new story based on a long-ago past they never knew; perhaps they are using stereotyped memories of television adventure shows as the jumping-off point for their learning. They may feel they are simply enacting a literal story, but they will in fact be operating in an aesthetic frame of their own making.

Occasionally a story will pose questions that might be employed to elicit spontaneous responses from listeners. A witch in a story might be interrogating passers-by about the whereabouts of a certain character or object. The storyteller, in role as the witch, might turn to a listener seated nearby and simply say something like, "Hawk, have you seen my sister's brooch?" Usually the listener will reply. Once a group has become accustomed to this set-up, responses gradually become easier and lead to interesting elaboration of the story. It is even possible that some spontaneous conversations will become part of the tale.

Exploring a Story through Drama

Enacting the Story (representing what we have experienced)

Enactment or dramatizing a story is the traditional method of combining story and drama. However, a simple recounting of the plot does not create drama. There must be a new discovery, a new learning, for drama to be happening during the enactment of a story. After the children read or hear the story, they can discuss it, and then decide how they would like to dramatize it. They must understand who they will be, where and when the story takes place, and what they are going to do. They then can begin the action and improvise the dialogue. Rather than recreating details and story line, they can use the issues, the themes, the characters or the conflict as a beginning for dramatic exploration. They may dramatize the problem of the action, or re-examine the incidents from a new perspective. We must create a new telling, using the concepts rather than the exact details of the story.

The children can retell the story in role as the characters or as witnesses to the events. They can explore the story from the different points of view of the characters.

A Ghost Story

The following anonymous poem was used with a Grade 2 class.

In a dark dark woods
there is a dark dark house

In the dark dark house
there is a dark dark stair

Down the dark dark stair
there is a dark dark cellar

In the dark dark cellar
there is a dark dark cupboard

In the dark dark cupboard
there is a dark dark bottle

In the dark dark bottle
there is a dark dark spirit

Slowly slowly the evil spirit P-U-S-H-E-S
out the cork. Now he F-L-O-A-T-S...

Out of the dark dark bottle
through the dark dark cupboard...

Out of the dark dark cupboard
through the dark dark cellar...

Out of the dark dark cellar
up the dark dark stair...

Out of the dark dark stair
through the dark dark house...

Out of the dark dark house
through the dark dark woods...

Out of the dark dark woods
into your dark...dark...pocket!

He's got you!

After a short discussion of the poem, the teacher showed the children *The Haunted House,* a three-dimensional, moving-picture book of monsters and ghosts. This elicited a lively response — exclamations of surprise and laughter — from the children. The teacher then read *In a Dark Dark House,* a book of the same theme appropriate for Hallowe'en.

With the children working in pairs, the teacher led the students through various rhythmic clappings and jumping games accompanied by chants. Eventually, the pairs joined other pairs and the children continued with the games in groups.

All the students then lay on the floor, shoulder to shoulder, and rolled across the room like waves on the ocean. This proved a very successful activity, and the children expressed a great deal of enjoyment and involvement in it.

Some simple dramatic exercises, done first in pairs and then in groups, followed. The initial poem was re-read, and the children were encouraged to make their individual responses to the story (e.g., "What is in the closet of the dark, dark house? Open the door and what do you discover? Pretend you are what is in the closet when your partner opens the door. Who will you be? What will you say?").

The class as a whole then began to dramatize the story. One child volunteered to be behind the door when it opened. The rest of the children developed their roles in response to the behaviour of the unknown person behind the door.

The first volunteer had lost her baby, and was searching for it. The children questioned her about her background and her present condition, and volunteered to assist in the search. Some children explained that they had entered the house because they heard weeping. The problem was resolved, eventually, and a new drama began, this time with the entire group behind the door, and the volunteer knocking.

Elaborating (building on the story's strengths)

After reading a story, children can elaborate upon the sub-textual information in the story — the stories within the story. A minor detail may provide the stimulus for an improvisation, or minor characters may be expanded as the children explore motivations and relationships. Questions the children raise as they probe for deeper insights into a situation can provide the stimulus for drama:

- exploring story incidents that are briefly described or hinted at;
- stopping the action of the story at a particular place or moment of time to examine its significance;
- building dramas based on questions and concerns of the children themselves engaging with the story to make new meanings.

The Magic Staff

A group of six-year-olds had listened to *Little Sister and the Month Brothers* by Beatrice Schenk de Regniers, read by their teacher. At the conclusion of the story, they displayed keen interest in a magic staff owned by the Month Brothers. With this staff, the brothers could change the weather in a given location on demand. The teacher permitted the children to pursue their interest in this aspect of the story. Over the next few days, they created staffs of rolled newspaper, then painted and decorated them. In the play corner, the staffs stimulated much spontaneous play. Eventually, the children wrote collectively a book of rules for the use of magic staffs. In the spontaneous play with the staffs, they often repeated moments from the original story. Taking note of this, the teacher developed a drama lesson, using other characters from the original story. Essentially the drama developed around the need of some characters in the story to borrow the powerful staff from the Month Brothers. In dealing with this problem, the children had a rewarding experience relating present circumstances to past memory of story characters and events. In contemplating the terrible responsibilities of owning an object so powerful, they were clarifying their understanding of human strengths and frailties.

Extending (stretching the story)

The children can use their imaginations to extend stories backwards into the past or forwards into the imagined future. Or, while reading a story, the teacher may stop at a point where various alternatives for action are presented and ask the children to develop the possibilities of these alternatives. The teacher may also add characters not found in the story and suggest that the children find ways to make them major players in the story.

- building upon the group's ideas of what might have happened in the story or what could happen next;
- building on the story's concepts by designing a new context for it, or placing it alongside other stories for comparison;
- problem-solving unresolved situations by extending the premise of the story.

The Eyes of the Dragon

Frequently, the children will want to continue a story if the ending doesn't seem completely tidy. It's not so much a new story in such cases as it is a reworking of story elements. In the case of Ed Young's *The Eyes of the Dragon*, a village has been left in ruins because of the stubbornness of the village magistrate. A wall around the village which affords much-needed protection has collapsed, destroying many homes and leaving the villagers in chaos. There are many implications about who is responsible, but the main thing is that the story ends with everything in a mess.

In one classroom, the children banded into groups, each group representing one main character in the story. The teacher, in role as an investigator dispatched by the Chinese Emperor, hot-seated each group in an attempt to get to the bottom of the situation and to help the villagers form a rebuilding plan. The work leaned heavily on the children's recall of actual and imagined events from the story. In the drama process of interviewing the villagers, it was agreed that the rebuilding of the wall should commence immediately. When it came time to decide who would do it, however, a situation not unlike the story of the Little Red Hen emerged. Some within the village, it seemed, were above manual labour and only wanted to supervise. Suddenly, a whole new story had developed.

Inventing (creating new stories from old ones)

Using a story as a basis, the children can explore additional problems related to it, or alter the events of the story to build a new one. They can invent their own story dramas from any implications for their own lives that they see in the story:

- using patterns from the story to create new stories;
- using characters from the story in other plot situations;
- using contexts and concepts from the story as the basis for new ones;

- developing incidents that did not occur in the story but might have;
- exploring a situation or a problem that parallels those developed in the story, creating an analogy.

Where the Wild Things Are

In *The Wild Things Go to School*, Cecily O'Neill, an authority on drama in education, writes about a classroom teacher she knows who took hold of drama and story and gave her children a powerful new tool for both making meaning collaboratively and bringing more meaning to a complex picture book. Note that the drama here results not in a formal theatrical production, but in a variety of activities.

> Sylvia is excited by the possibility of using drama across the curriculum. She is interested in exploring ways in which drama can illuminate and enrich her broader purposes as a teacher. One of her continuing concerns is finding ways to improve her students' reading skills. Using a favourite book — *Where the Wild Things Are* — she devised a simple but most effective drama framework to address these essential teacher concerns.
>
> Working in role as "Max," who is now an adult, she told the class that she was very concerned about the Wild Things. For years, since Max's first visit to the Wild Things, he had been writing them letters, postcards and Christmas cards, but without ever receiving a reply. At last, he had sailed to see them once again. When he reached the island, he could see from a distance the Wild Things sitting dejectedly in a circle. In the middle of the circle was a huge heap of all the letters and cards he had written them. Suddenly, Max realised the truth. The Wild Things could not read. Now Max had come to the children to ask their help with this problem. Grown-ups were no use, since they couldn't see the Wild Things. Would they teach the creatures to read? The children eagerly accepted the challenge. Much time was spent finding out where the Wild Things lived, and planning how to travel there and transport the creatures back to the classroom. Mapping, designing, problem-solving and decision-making were all part of this phase of the work. The children took great pains to prepare the classroom to receive the Wild Things. They considered the kind of environment which would be comfortable for the creatures. The classroom was transformed to look as much like a jungle as possible, and everything was labeled by the children to assist the Wild Things with beginning reading skills. The children made large paper Wild Things, and Sylvia paired the students so that they could support each other in their reading. The children were able to call upon her in the role as "Max" to resource and assist them in their teaching task. The children made Big Books for the creatures, and prepared other reading materials which they hoped would appeal to them. They found clever ways of pretending that their Wild Things did work which they actually did themselves. The Wild Things wrote several books, and some read them aloud to the class in squeaky voices. Each child kept a Project Record Book for their Wild Thing, in which the creatures wrote about what they did each day. Lessons in classroom behaviour, morality and even appropriate cuisine for the Wild Things arose as the work progressed. At one point, Sylvia invited the Reading Consultant for the area to come and work with the children in order to reinforce their instructional strategies.

At the beginning of this unit, Sylvia had asked the children to list the strategies they used to help themselves read. At the end of the work she did the same, and the children's list of strategies was more extensive, much more creative and clearly demonstrated an understanding of the reading/writing connection. They had acquired a considerable number of new strategies to improve their own reading skills. It seems clear that the children's experience as "teachers" in the drama reinforced their sense of themselves as learners: it brought the process of learning to read into explicit focus, but the activity remained one in which they possessed both status and competence. They actively promoted their own learning as well as that of the imaginary Wild things, and both inside and outside the drama they grew in skills and confidence.

From Poetry into Drama

For a language conference, we were asked to conduct a demonstration lesson on the creative thinking that might grow from a story, and for our own interest we selected a narrative poem that might appear difficult for the Grade 1 class we were going to work with. However, one of us would read the poem to them in the voice of the character telling the story, and the other would be the teacher in role building the drama with the children. The poem is one of atmosphere and feeling, and contains much subtext for exploration.

Our Pond

The pond in our garden
Is murky and deep
And lots of things live there
That slither and creep.

Like diving bell spiders
And great ramshorn snails
And whirligig beetles
And black snappertails.

There used to be goldfish
That nibbled my thumb,
But now there's just algae
And sour, crusty scum.

There used to be pondweed
With fizzy green shoots,
But now there are leeches
And horrible newts.

One day when my football
Rolled in by mistake
I tried to retrieve it
By using a rake.

But as I leaned over
A shape from the ooze
Bulged up like a nightmare
And lunged at my shoes.

I ran back in shouting,
But everyone laughed
And said I was teasing
Or else I was daft.

But I know what happened
And when I'm asleep
I dream of those creatures
That slither and creep

The diving bell spiders
And great ramshorn snails
And whirligig beetles
And black snappertails.

Richard Edwards

It was interesting to see that the children at first were certain that the character who had read the poem had really seen nothing in the pond. They mentioned that he perhaps had had a daydream or that he was prone to exaggeration. However, the character's belief in the creature prompted one child to explain that perhaps it had been a shadow. When asked what might have caused that shadow, the children offered many suggestions, the most interesting of which was Tanya's description of a birdhouse in the next yard "looking like something on the surface of the pond, and when a bird left the birdhouse, the shadow seemed to move inside the water."

Then Bob, as the storyteller, still in role, asked one child if he wanted to see the pool with him, and the child agreed and the two went hand in hand to a corner of the room. On their return, the child announced to the others: "I saw the thing in the pool." He was of course questioned by the children, and the mystery and the drama began to deepen. Most children expressed the view that the creature existed only in the storyteller's imagination, but others volunteered to examine the pool for themselves. Two or three children accompanied the storyteller to the pool each time, and on their return explained that they too had seen the creature. When asked to describe it, they used words like "shadowy," "oozing," "dark," "slithery." In role the storyteller was very calm and very certain that he had seen the creature, and those children who had gone with him to the pool assured us that they had as well.

David, the teacher in role, questioned the storyteller and the others about their ideas, and stated his doubts about anyone having seen anything. He pressed the children who had not gone with the storyteller to question those who had, and he talked to those who had gone about their experiences.

Near the end of the lesson, the teacher asked the storyteller to retell the experience of the pond, and he read the poem once more. During the final reflection, only one child remained who felt that the storyteller had seen nothing but shadows.

It was a fascinating experience to watch these six-year-olds gradually wander inside this complex story poem through roleplaying. As we noted earlier, in planning our lesson, we decided that one of us would share the poem, and the other would guide the children, but we were not sure how the process would actually work until the children began to respond. As we listened, we could sense the direction the journey would take, and we began a process of following and leading — a negotiation in role and out of role — that was developing as the children talked about their reactions to this strange story of the pond.

Reading Aloud

Traditionally, in a reading lesson, children have read stories aloud in order to check for pronunciation and syntactic comprehension. Often, the oral reading preceded discussion or the written answering of comprehension questions — testing questions. However, the skills embedded in oral interpretation are complex, to say the least, and for many children, oral reading has not led to deeper or stronger interpretation of the print, but to word-calling and to correcting the pronunciation of others in the group. The repeated reading aloud of a story as a rote exercise may even decrease a child's understanding of the meaning and appreciation of the story and the words. For these and other reasons, reading aloud by children has been abandoned by some dedicated teachers, and yet oral interpretation, when done well, can improve all the skills of comprehension, lead to revelation for the reader and strengthen the grasp of a particular interpretation on the part of the listener.

Without opportunity to interrogate the story, to rub up against it, to notice how others are feeling and wondering, to question private beliefs, to expand information and to hear the voices of print struggling for freedom, the child will be sharing print aloud for no learning reason. A few children can decode the text phonetically, but comprehend almost nothing. Even these, especially these, need occasions for coming to grips with the meat of the story before attempting to share their knowledge out loud. The teller and the told are each precious in this process of reading aloud. Sometimes, it is the reader who is also listening, learning through the ear and the eye at the same time.

What models are there for reading aloud?

- A parent who has read alongside the child throughout his or her life;
- a teacher who shares what she is personally reading, who may share some lines and excerpts;
- a teacher who delights in reading fine stories to children each and every day;
- a teacher who tells stories to the class, owning them, making them personal for the listener;
- a teacher who sings with the children, letting the story tunes fill their ears;
- a teacher who encourages reading aloud only when there is an audience who wants to listen.

Reading aloud has been the lifeblood of our work for forty years. We read, they read, we read together, we echo each other, we make dialogue into script, we chant, we sing, we demonstrate, we share moments, we delight in words, we repeat, we whisper, we shout, we read and move our bodies, we read and clap our hands, we read to those who can't or don't, we read what they don't have or can't see, we read to reveal information we have found, we read to make a point, we read together as a ritual of belonging, we read from our memories, without print, we read to hear the sounds of language, we read to give others our own print ideas, we read to change direction and refocus, we read to bring together bits and pieces into broader themes, we read to find the voices deep within the well, we read to raise our own voices in tribute to literacy.

We read aloud what we've written, excerpts from other stories that we loved or wondered about, words that touch us or puzzle us, tales from before, stories about today and tomorrow, episodes from people's lives, poems that cry out for sounds in the air, letters from friends, stories about places where we have never wandered, stories about dogs and horses and mothers and granddads and eccentrics and children and school and city and countryside, stories of hope and death and wonder and fantasy. We read short stories and long stories and chapters that build up the tension for days. We read stories from album covers and music sheets, blurbs about writers from the backs of book jackets, titles, reviews, and recommendations. We read aloud, we fill the classroom with the voices of our ancestors, our friends, our authors, our poets, our documents, our native people, our researchers, our journalists, our ad writers. We story aloud.

Can we as teachers give children the strengths required for oral reading so that they will approach the process with interest and excitement, accepting the challenge of bringing someone else's words to life, and the risk of discovering a means of communicating learning? Perhaps this is the most complicated and sophisticated of all response modes. Teachers need to re-examine their motives and strategies for including or excluding oral reading in the language programs of their classes.

Opportunities for Reading Aloud

If children have access to models of reading aloud, they will want to participate. We can encourage them in many ways:

1. Children can join in by reading songs, verses and poems aloud.
2. They can participate in the choral speaking of poems and rhythmic stories, safely anonymous from the critical ears of those who might hinder the process.
3. They can read big book stories, or favourite lines from selections on overhead transparencies and chart paper.
4. They can read their own writings aloud in small groups only after editing their print to permit ease in reading.
5. They can work with a buddy from an older class, someone who will offer an experienced shoulder to lean on as they read to each other, and delve deeply into the context of the story as they find ways to bring it to life.
6. They can read the dialogue of a story in groups as if it were from a script. The narrator will give them clues as to how to interpret the words. They can share excerpts from story novels with others who have not read the material, so that the listeners will be attentive.
7. They can read aloud sentences, phrases and words that are useful in proving a point during story discussion, responding with the words of others to support their own ideas.
8. They can read aloud findings from their research activities to other interested children. Perhaps different groups have explored various aspects of a theme or topic, and want to hear from each other to

expand their knowledge. They can transfer their findings to overhead transparencies or large charts and share the information by reading aloud. They can read aloud inside the drama frame, using words that they have created through roleplay, rules, statements, findings — or words they have found in excerpts, letters, documents, tales. This role reading gives added strength to the oral interpretation; belief and commitment often transcend any limitation or difficulty with reading print.

9. They can read scripts aloud in small groups, first reading silently, then exploring the concepts, finding the voices. Better to leave concentrated teaching to whole-class activities. The groups can tape-record their scripts for others to listen to.

10. They can dramatize poems and excerpts using the words of others, but, through interpretive improvisation, bring to them movement and belief. These "minimal scripts" offer opportunity for partner, small group and whole-class exploration. Situations can be added, characters can be changed, music can be incorporated. The children may want to commit passages to memory, the ultimate act of oral interpretation.

11. They can chant, sing, shout, call and respond alternate lines or sections of a story. At the conclusion of a particular theme or unit, they can read interesting or significant findings — poems that touched them, excerpts that made connections, quotations from novels that represent universal truths, personal writings from journals or writing folders that they feel will have special appeal for their class. The ritual of sharing and summarizing is vital to oral reading in many aspects of tribal life. We can incorporate this power into classroom teaching.

12. Readers' theatre is a technique that allows the children to dramatize narration — selections from novels, short stories, picture books, poems — instead of reading aloud scripted material.
   The children can have one person read the narration, others the dialogue speeches, or they can explore who should read which line. For example, a character who speaks dialogue may also read the information in the narration that refers to him or her. Several children can read narration as a chorus.

13. Story theatre is another technique that allows children to dramatize material other than scripts. As well as interpreting the dialogue and the narration aloud, the participants can also play out all the actions and movements in the story. Simple narratives, such as those found in myth, fable, legend, and folktale from the oral tradition, are best suited for story theatre.

Reading, Drama and the Novel

A Grade 7 class was working with us on *I Am the Cheese* by Robert Cormier, a complicated text consisting of a seemingly random and yet cumulative series of transcripts between an interviewer and an interviewee. Because we were new to this class and wanted to ensure an appropriate comfort level, we decided to work in small groups for the first hour-long session. With six copies of the book, we were able to break into groups of five. Each group chose a reader who then read aloud a particular excerpt that we had marked, and no more. Then the books were closed while the members of each group discussed simply: "What is happening in your excerpt?" The transcripts were brief, minimal scripts, as seen in this sample:

T: Tell me about the telephone calls. (10-second interval.)
A: I have a feeling you already know about them. I have a feeling you know everything, even my blank spots.
T: Then, why should I make you go through it all? Why should I carry on this charade?
A: I don't know.
T: You disappoint me. Can't you think of the one person who will benefit? (5-second interval.)
A: Me. Me. Me. That's what you said at the beginning. But I never asked for it. I never asked to benefit by it. (4-second interval.)
A: I have a headache.
T: Don't retreat now. Don't retreat. Tell me about the phone calls your mother made. (5-second interval.)
A: There really isn't very much to tell.

At first, the children had little to say, since the text gave almost no information. However, as the discussion proceeded, questions arose, and the children began asking to hear their particular excerpt read again. It was a frustrating exercise, because they knew that inside the book might be all the answers to their questions. And yet they played along with us, working within what we had called a story puzzle. We then called all the groups together, and began to list on chart paper the information that each group had gleaned from its own marked source in the novel. As the details emerged it was amazing to see the excellent reading that had been accomplished. However, one child asked to see another group's selection, and we had the various groups share with each other by having two groups exchange information by reading the excerpts aloud as a dialogue, until all groups had met each other. This took the remaining time in the first session.

At the beginning of the second session, the children volunteered information they had remembered from the previous session, as well as ideas they had discussed during the week. The list of suggestions was long, and many strong directions were beginning to emerge. However, they had not identified the exact relationship of the characters in the book. The period was over, and on the way out the door, two girls came running back into the room shouting: "It's the CIA in Washington! He is being interrogated! The boy's parents were assassinated!" The entire class congregated around us demanding an answer, and we offered the six copies of the novel to volunteers, who snatched them from our hands.

The final session began and ended with their questions, about the book, abandoned children, interrogation, brainwashing, government control agencies, truth and fiction. They had talked their way into making their own stories from one novel.

Writing Our Own Stories

When they write from inside the world of the story, when what they write is drawn from or stimulated by the original source, we give children a huge repertoire of resources that they can draw upon, and we also give them a set of constraints. This type of "dependent authorship" lets students look at their own work and the work of the story, all at once. The connection between reading and writing has been evident in the classroom for a long time. What does writing do for the reader? What does reading do for the writer?

For most children, writing has been used as a follow-up to what has been read. Story patterns and story ideas have suggested the content of the resulting composition. The story has sometimes been forgotten, acting only as a stimulus for beginning and structuring the ideas for writing. As well, many children have spent hours answering comprehension questions, but never consider the writing of their answers as an act of writing. As they relate, retell, restate, find evidence for, sequence, infer and judge, they are oblivious of how they are structuring and recording their answers. Even when taking up the questions, few teachers or children pay attention to the composition involved in the answers. New projects that are suggested, such as "book reporting" activities, and all types of work cards and centres that ask the child to respond to the story by writing, too often take the child away from the response mode to one of inventing, virtually a language activity. This is not to say that these types of activities are not of value. But they do not exhaust the possibilities of story as a wonderful springboard for writing: written responses to story will reveal and alter comprehension; follow-up storying activities can integrate language learning and help children to express, organize and communicate their ideas and questions. All acts of languaging are interrelated, but story should hold a special place in the child's development. The writing activities that generate other stories must be true learning situations for both the child as reader and the child as writer. The teacher can assist the child, but the child must be storying through writing.

The problems involved in writing down stories are varied and complex. For many children, encoding the story in print seems an insurmountable task. Very few teachers put themselves through such rigorous activity. The students know they will be judged not just on their storying strength but on their ability to put it down in print. Might they then forego the story for the form? Is there a danger that their tellings will take second place to their concern with the formalities of print? Is it possible that in our attempts to teach writing we may destroy story? It is a complicated task.

Today, we have computers and writing software programs to help us edit and revise and publish our writing. Children can now find support for putting down their ideas in print. Of course, we also use in our work sheets of newsprint, markers, chalk boards, art materials — all to capture thoughts in the midst of action. We can use these written records as the basis for further written work at another time.

What stories do children write down? Real ones from their own experiences; semi-real ones they have heard or latched onto; memories that filter through time; dreams that may seem very real; fantasies that carry them out and beyond the real world; fictions that let them take part in any event they can imagine or conjure up; literary stories of all types using all patterns: monologues, tall tales, legends, poems, dialogues, updates. Could writing our story be like painting our story, where the process is embedded inside the final product? Editing a story must be a separate process from storying, unless we can see revision as a continually changing version of our story. Can we retrain ourselves as teachers to listen to the stories that the children want to tell? Through pre-writing activities, we can enable and support them in the search for forms and structures for sharing their stories. There are so many reasons to write and revise. However, it is storying that we must be concerned with, that we must encourage and strengthen. Each child is a potential teller of tales.

Children's writing draws from the content of the stories they have met — concepts, characters, styles, and patterns — both consciously and unconsciously. They begin by borrowing, and then they manipulate the ideas and conventions of story. They can begin by borrowing events, themes, issues, words, patterns and characters, and continue to expand their own story hoards. When they connect stories to the larger body of literature, children are developing their sense of story. Comparing several stories by one author or books on the same subject or theme, so that children can place what they have read or heard in relation to other stories, gives them the chance to develop personal preference and the ability to discern and critique. More is better. They are developing their story frames, widening their expectations of what a story can be, how it can be constructed, how it can develop.

> My granddad was born on May 11th, 1891 in Canton, China. He came to this country by boat and landed in Victoria, B.C. on January 22nd, 1911. He came here with his brother in search of a new life.
>
> Life was tough for the two brothers. And life became tougher when they had to pay the Head Tax to legally stay in Canada. In 1923 that amounted to a lot of money in those days. Grandad met his first wife who was a nanny for a rich family also from China. His first wife passed away at a very young age in Montreal.
>
> Granddad and his brother moved from city to city in the laundry business. They had a business in Vancouver, Montreal, Toronto and Ottawa. Many Chinese people started in the laundry business because it didn't take much money to start. This was before machines, so all it took was hard work, soap and water.
>
> Granddad was lonely for a long time because Chinese men were not allowed to sponsor families to come to Canada because of the Chinese Expulsion Act. This Act was not changed until the early 1950s. In 1954, Granddad went to Hong Kong to visit and meet my grandmom there. They got married in 1955. They came back to Canada and shortly after they settled in Ottawa and Toronto and eventually moved to northern Ontario. They lived in Kirkland Lake and Kapuskasing and eventually

Hornpayne, where he was in the restaurant business servicing mining communities.

My dad was born in Hearst, Ontario because Hornpayne was so small and there was no hospital. They later moved to Toronto when Granddad retired in his early 70s. He lived in Toronto until he died in 1996 at 104 years of age.

Ciara Hong, Grade 4, as told by her family

The stories children hear and read give them ideas for writing, and that writing in turn can be used for sharing their insights into the stories they have experienced. Revealing our understanding of a story through writing lets us then link two vital processes together so that we can share what is inside our minds. We verbalize and mediate our feelings in our writing. We can become active storyers who begin to understand themselves as both readers and writers.

It can also be very interesting to compare our own ideas for writing with those created by professional authors. A poem by Michael Rosen demonstrates this with a powerful sense of the way we use language in everyday contexts:

Shut Your Mouth When You're Eating

Shut your mouth when you're eating.
I am, Dad. It is shut.
I can see it isn't. I can hear it isn't.
What about his mouth? You can see everything in his mouth.
He's only two. He doesn't know any better.
You can see all his peas and tomato sauce.
That's none of your business.

(2 minutes go by) Dad.
Yes.
Your mouth's open. Shut your mouth when you're eating.
It is shut, thank you very much.
I can see it isn't, Dad. I can see all the food in there.
Look that's my business, OK?
Peas, gravy, spuds, everything.
Look, you don't want to grow up to be as horrible as your father do you?
Answer that, smartyboots.

Rosen's scripted monologues and dialogues are so close to the lives of most children that speaking them aloud seems entirely natural. In fact, timing, pacing, intonation and rhythm are caught almost instantly. The children's own verse from street and playground can also be examined and compared with the work of poets and with older works from the oral tradition. Moving through and about this great medley of sound and voice and rhythm and story cannot help but keep the sounds of language ringing forever in the ears of the children we teach.

Today's writing curricula stress the active use of writing rather than exercises about writing. In some classrooms, traditional motivations for writing have dealt not with an inner compulsion or felt need, but only with the completion of creative writing tasks. When the writing is embedded in a context that has a personal significance for the writer, writing skills will be enhanced. The writer will work with genuine feeling and thoughtfulness, exploring meaning through both content and form. Writers/participants embody their feelings and ideas, learning not only to express themselves but to rethink, reassess, restructure, and re-examine themselves in the light of their own growth, perhaps even with an understanding of the reading audience and its needs.

Writing In Role

Drama can assist us in several ways in helping children engage in writing. The imaginative involvement that arises in drama can in turn be a powerful stimulus for writing. That writing can serve several different purposes in building and developing an imaginative thematic unit. The best language work grows over an extended period, during which children have time and incentive to work their way in to refocus and change directions and to edit and present their creations to trusted and accepting others. By working in role, children are attempting to change perspective and move into inventive worlds and unfamiliar contexts.

Within drama, the students can explore all the writing strategies — free writing, journals, interviews, brainstorming, lists, letter writing; creating announcements, proclamations and petitions; reporting about events within the drama; designing advertisements and brochures; inventing questionnaires and important documents; and writing narrative stories that are part of or that are conjured up by the story told. As well, many opportunities are provided for collective writing, in which groups collaborate on a mutual enterprise. For example, they can cooperate in collecting data, organizing information, revising and editing, all in a learning context.

From a story in the George and Martha series by James Marshall, the children in one Grade 2 class decided to write advice to George. Most of the selections begin in the first person, although there was no instruction from the teacher.

> I advise you to make your own food so you won't say to each other I don't like this and go to restronts alot and if one of you are ill ask him or her what you would like and how they wont it made thats what I say.

> I understand your problem you ought to tell Martha about the soup or just say I don't want that today. If you feel that way about Martha. Why don't you marry then it would be easyer to tell her don't you think. I am sure you will get along with each other. I would try some more flavors of soup it could be tasty.

> You should not be angry you should tell them to be friends maybe marry live together. Or spend a holiday together. Buy presents for each other by happy enjoy life. Meet people. They should never disagree.

> I advised George to tell Martha every time if there was any trouble. I advised Martha never to give Ceorge Split Pea Soup again.

> All you have to do is to tell Martha the truth because she will find out later. You should live together because will make a nice couple. Martha would make you cook.

A group of nine-year-olds had been working with Kermit Krueger's telling of the folktale "The Golden Swans." They had improvised the incident that occurs when the stranger is forced to build a statue in memory of the swan, and created these warnings to be carved thereon:

Death to those who comes here to kill. The hunter who killed our ansestors cared this. The man who killed the swan has carved the swan for us. This is a trubute to show what happened to the ansesters when one hunter came along an distroyed them. They were in the form of a swan.

Do not tuch the swans or els. Because they men so mytch to us.

Never kill a thing.

Those who kill our swans shall be put to work. Those who kill in this village shall be punished. To the passers and villagers that live in the village. You have kill the swan and have done evil.

We do not kill. And those who do kill will do work and they will not finish until it is completely finished. Never kill a golden swan without permission, for the story says never.

People who are near read this. This statue is a dead swan; it is alone for all to remember.

In the following letters by students playing the role of the stranger in the tale, the children show strong role identification, as well as an understanding of the feelings of the hunter and the consequences of his deed.

In their discussion they decided that the story was set in Vietnam. The letters vary between the formality of the hunter who has committed the crime and the informality of people away from home writing a friendly letter. This mix of the actual and the invented demonstrates the variety of meanings that must be a part of the learning with a group of children.

Dear brother I have found this strange town with the name of Viet Nam there is a story about some golden swans which are really spirits when you grow up please come and you might even see them. They were made by Indra's god come when you are older.

Dear daughter and son,

I am writing to you to tell you I am ok. I am in Viet Nam in a little village. It is very strange in this little village. Then one day I was walking in a deep forest when I saw a lake and some golden swans I ran and caught one. When I felt it died. And the people of the village were angry with me. I said I was sorry, but they still are angry. I have pondered for many days, and I have thought of a idea. I have built a statue of a swan, and the people have lost their angryness.

from your father,

p.s. Hope you are keeping well.

Dear Son

It is very strange in this place. I killed a golden swan and all the towns people were very mad with me. I hope you are ok. They played war with me for been a hunter because they had no hunters in that land. I hope I will be coming home soon. I just sit here thinking about the crime I caused. I know no one here. I hope mum will send me clen clothes.

Parallel Reading

After a story experience, children can meet more stories that illuminate, clarify or open up the original narrative.

We may begin with one particular story with a class, but before long, the children have found a dozen more, some hidden in the recesses of their story minds, some discovered in the library, some invented through storytelling sessions, and others created collaboratively through story-building activities. As teachers, we also add our own selections, some to be read or told aloud, others to be left on a table to be read by volunteers. One story gives birth to a thousand.

Story Sets

It can be an exciting adventure for children to meet literary versions of a story they think they know. Suddenly, their preconceptions are jolted, and they move into an altered state, caught in a web of changing perception, noticing every minute difference. The story brain is engaged.

When children experience two or more stories that are related in some way, their understanding of each is altered and enriched by the other as they make connections between their expanding lives and the stories. Often one story prepares the reader for another one, facilitating the understanding of the subsequent story. And of course, each new story sheds light on past story experiences, creating a changing view of the stories in the child's story repertoire.

Children can meet all kinds of different stories and then focus on similarities and differences; individuals can each read a different story, and then share their understandings and findings. There are many ways to organize the sharing of different but related stories — comparison charts, which demonstrate particular characteristics within different categories, samples of specific language peculiarities, emotional responses, analyses of artistic interpretations, variations in story structures, settings, cultures or resolutions. There are always different findings and insights to be shared.

As we journey along story pathways we may suddenly find a story we passed just recently reappearing with new life, new vitality (stories connecting stories, and stories being recreated).

Owl Trouble

Crows detest you.
With his sharp eyes, one spots you,
lets out a 'caw' that tells the others you are here.
Gathering around you
perching as close as possible cawing at the top of their black voices,
tormenting until you can stand it no longer.

You fly off with a scream followed by this noisy black mob, this tail of tormentors.
Owl, you frighten me.
Owl, you fascinate me.

David Booth

A momentary observation, "Crows detest you," an act of panic, "You fly off with a scream," a statement of emotion, "Owl, you fascinate me." Resonances of stories from all over the world cry out their "owl lore."

Why Hens Are Afraid of Owls

Once upon a time, hens had dances every Saturday night. They employed Mr. Owl for a fiddler. He was always careful to go away before daylight so that the hens might not see his big eyes. The last time he fiddled for them, daylight caught him, and when the hens had a look at his eyes they were frightened into fits and went squalling out of the room.

Ever since then, the hen cannot even bear the shadow of an owl.

Roger Abrahams,
African American Folktales

Owl hiding his eyes. How like the story of Owl in the wonderful collection of Haitian folktales, *The Magic Orange Tree*, by Diane Wolkstein, where "Owl thought he was ugly" so he moved freely only in shadow and darkness until he fell in love. Shadow and darkness. The fate of Owl in "The Hedge King," retold by the Brothers Grimm, where Owl incurs the wrath of all the birds when he fails to keep as prisoner the tiny "hedge bird" who has just cheated in the contest to name a king of the birds. As punishment, Owl is banished to the night world and badgered by all birds if he shows his face by day. Shows his face by day. Certainly something that Owl in Ted Hughes's story "How the Owl Became" can never do again. Here is played out a macabre tale in which Owl, a master of cunning and deceit, almost succeeds in enslaving the entire feather-and-claw population. The incredible exodus led by Owl, through underground rabbit warrens, makes for compelling reading and telling.

The Man Who Could Call Down Owls is a powerful tale of revenge, as Charles Mikolaycak's black and white illustrations paint a world of feathers and night. When the owls attack the imposter who has murdered the one who could call them down, the story gruesomely demonstrates the strange and precarious balance of nature.

Why are there owls in these stories? Are they themes and metaphors, allegories, ideas or birds — or all of the above?

As teachers, we can help the children classify or categorize stories by genre, type, theme, or story attributes. Consider the options:

Variations of the same folktale	*Dawn* by Molly Bang. *The Crane Wife* by Katherine Paterson. Adaptations of a Japanese legend.

Cultural variants of the same tale	"The Invisible Boy" in Alden Nowlan's *Nine Micmac Legends*. An Indian Cinderella story.
Different versions of the same story	"Tom Poker" in Allan Garner's *A Bag of Moonshine*. Who is stronger — Sun, Wind or Cloud?
Same story pictured by different illustrators	*The Wild Swans* by Hans Christian Andersen. Illustrated by Angela Barrett. *The Wild Swans*. Illustrated by Helen Stratton.
Stories with similar structures	*The Cat Who Loved to Sing* by Nonny Hogrogian. *Hattie and the Fox* by Mem Fox. Cumulative structures.
Stories on a particular theme or topic	*Ananci Spiderman* by James Berry. Stories of the West Indian trickster/hero.
Tales of specific genres — ballads, etc.	*Proud Knight, Fair Lady* by Naomi Lewis (trans.). The Twelve Lays of Marie de France.
Books by one author or illustrator	*Collected Stories* by Richard Kennedy. Illustrated by Marcia Sewall.
Stories with the same characters	*Tales of the Early World* by Ted Hughes. God is portrayed as an artist creating the earth's creatures.
Stories from the same culture	*Three Indian Princesses* by Jamila Gavin. Three heroines from the folktales of India.
Stories with similar motifs	*The Buffalo Boy and the Weaver Girl* by Mary Alice Downie. *The Selchie Girl* by Susan Cooper. *The Buffalo Woman* by Paul Goble. Taboo: giving garment back to supernatural wife.

The chart on the next page examines one motif in story — animals — and then explores the many classifications that can emerge. Children can read and listen to selections from one category, or groups can compare stories for attributes in order to classify them.

Story Art

For many children, the visual arts (we include in this category drawing, painting, collage, work with construction paper, papier mache, and so on) are their sole means of representing thoughts and feelings. Some children naturally think in visual terms. Others, who are unable to write responses — because of their literacy development, anxiety, lack of

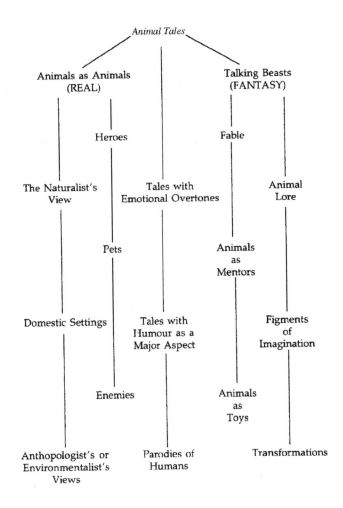

Animal Tales

Animals as Animals (REAL) — Talking Beasts (FANTASY)

Heroes — Fable

The Naturalist's View — Tales with Emotional Overtones — Animal Lore

Pets — Animals as Mentors

Domestic Settings — Tales with Humour as a Major Aspect — Figments of Imagination

Enemies — Animals as Toys

Anthopologist's or Environmentalist's Views — Parodies of Humans — Transformations

self-worth or attitude — can and often will express their ideas visually in a non-print medium. The results can then be used as "notes" or points for group discussion, or just as a personal expressive response. The teacher can observe what the child chooses to "say" — the details that seemed significant, the content of the art, the feeling that is suggested, the style used for representation. Through further discussion, in a student/teacher dialogue or in small groups, the child may further reveal and explain, and we can help the child clarify, modify, support and extend the story. Writing is a medium with strengths and weaknesses. Visual arts may offer a different mode of expression and communication, spontaneous and unedited, one that flows out of the story experience as a natural form.

Our concern here is the storying; artistic development is an important byproduct, but not the primary concern for our purposes.

In his book *Draw Me a Story*, Bob Steele draws our attention to the drawings that children create as they tell their stories through their art. Because their literacy skills are still developing, children intuitively use the medium most likely to satisfy their needs: words for practical communication, and drawing for expressing the more subtle and complex thoughts and feelings which are beyond their ability to express in words, as a language to articulate and represent their feelings and emotions. Drawings contain levels of aesthetic energy rarely matched in a child's verbal expression. Drawings are an attempt to make sense of the world in whatever medium is available and most easily used.

Children draw what they see, what they know and what they feel. Drawing encourages empathic identification whereby children not only record what they know, but completely identify with it. They draw selectively, according to their feelings, exaggerating and distorting forms that are of particular importance to them. Drawing also offers an alternative language for children who have problems with literacy and academic subjects.

When they draw, children may relieve the emotional tensions of negative situations or celebrate life and give expression to positive emotions. Drawing provides a medium for sloughing off negative feelings and diminishing overt aggression. When children are battered by emotional storms, drawing can provide an opportunity to restore balance. It can reflect a child's frustration at not being able to think and communicate effectively with words.

Bob Steele writes:

Many teachers recognize drawing as an aid to literacy but rarely as a language in its own right. Formula art (providing images for colouring in, making uniform craft objects and seasonal decorations) makes no use at all of children's creativity, yet is still widely practiced, even when authentic drawing is considered part of the language program. The arts are as much cognitive as affective and are beneficial to perception, intellect, memory, imagination and judgement. The arts are the only subjects that integrate intellectual and affective modes of learning. From the multitude of perceptions children experience, only a few will be articulated through language. Drawing is not only the unrecognized language but the misunderstood language.

Images of Mother Goose

One simple strategy is to use collage to free children from the need for print or artistic skill. A Grade 4 classroom had a large supply of colourful magazines available for the following lesson. The teacher began by reading the nursery rhyme "Hannah Bantry" aloud.

> Hannah Bantry
> In the Pantry
> Gnawing on a mutton bone,
> How she gnawed it,
> How she clawed it,
> When she found herself alone.

As the teacher reread the poem, the children were asked to imagine Hannah in their minds — when she lived, what she looked like, what she was wearing, why she was eating in such a fashion, what she did, why she waited to be alone, why the lines had lived for so many years. Then, individually and silently, without conferring with each other, the children were to create a picture of Hannah Bantry, caught in the act, as if by a camera. They were to use collage — looking through magazines for pictures or pieces of pictures, ripping them out carefully and gluing them to a sheet of cardboard. The children were asked to use as many symbols as possible in creating their visuals, to represent Hannah's life with whatever images they thought could suggest and interpret it for a viewer.

When the portraits were complete, the children mounted their creations with masking tape across the blackboard. Then they examined all the pieces of art and began to notice similarities and differences.

As a class the children began to classify and categorize the faces: those that seemed frightened, those that appeared lonely, those that loved food, those that were happy, and so on. The children were examining responses to the story poem, building a world of personal interpretation and adding to their own singular visions by sharing perceptions, helping each other examine critically and coming to understand the general principles of building bigger story worlds through interaction.

Seeing What We Think

In this example of one child's collage of the father in *My Dad Lives in a Downtown Hotel* by Peggy Mann, you can see the interpretation he has created, a strong representation of that father; a picture story of what the child has thought and felt. Children can respond to story visually through picture making, crafts and games, or filmmaking. The teacher can provide materials for artistic work, and help children to think about their responses to a story in order to focus their questions and reactions through painting and modeling. Collaborative efforts can draw children together as they plan and work through their ideas and feelings about the story. Sometimes the art can be used to further the story

response — within a role, as illustration of the writing, as an opportunity to share perceptions. Picture books present a wonderful source for artistic response — the medium used, the style and format, and the point of view of the illustrator can all stimulate non-print activity.

The popularity of television and computers may have resulted in children who are far more adept at responding to visual symbols than to the written word. Whether this is true or not, visual response is an important means of interpreting the world. An appreciation of literature can be developed and motivation increased if we promote the constant harnessing of literature and the visual — television, film, cartoon, and the children's own work as picture-makers.

Children can assemble materials that relate to the story or stories they are exploring, objects mentioned in the text — collections, maps, facsimiles of journals, letters, advertisements, songs, clothes of the appropriate time. The research that the children collect can add to the context of the story either before or after its being shared, and the information presented can be an experience in itself.

Response through Visual Art

Why should we deny child-artists this medium for storytelling? There are many literacies, and many modes of making meaning. Are artists not thinkers? Should we deprive young people of the game of thought, freed of print restrictions, problem-solving using symbol systems with paint and brush? Perhaps the little drawing at the bottom of the child's page of story writing does not represent doodles or time fillers, but rather represents the heart of the response, a zap of inspired illumination. Children should have access to visual arts materials as media for their response repertoire. We want children to explore worlds of meanings in all dimensions. Their art can lead to new insights for artist and receiver, for the teacher-patron and for the children who share with each other.

1. Visual arts can be used to prepare for a story session. A special puppet, a significant prop, a carefully executed illustration can set the scene, provide immediate involvement and personalize the telling.
2. Children can sketch ideas as they read or listen to a story, or afterwards; their sketches can be used as jumping-off points for other activities, such as discussions, journals, comparisons of viewpoints, looking at sequences of story constructs.
3. A story told or shared without pictures to complement it can be the starting point for artistic interpretation. If the stress is on interpretation — an act of composing — rather than on the craftsmanship of the endeavour, the child will develop his own picture book, and take his place as a visual storyteller.
4. Children can create visuals cooperatively or collaboratively, negotiating their ideas and images, building on story response. Murals, dramas, cartoon strips, class-books, constructions using Lego toys, can all be part of the response.

5. Maps, charts and graphs may lead to an in-depth analysis or synthesis of a story. As the children grapple with representing ideas, details, events and significances, they may come to understand the power of story with graphic involvement.

6. An illustrated story may suggest to the reader a medium or technique to be used in the response. *Owl Lake* by Tejima cries out for printmaking on heavy, quality paper. The content can be determined by the interpretation of the children. Will they revisit the owl family? Are birds of their region to be compared? Does Nature's unrelenting violence catch their fancy? Will they leave a margin around their pages, as Tejima does on some? Are they going to spread the wings across the whole of the paper? Will they hide the owls in the trees or create close-up views of their eyes? Are there other picture books, informational or fictional, to examine for assistance in developing a response? Teachers must provide materials, techniques and direction; children will develop their own responses.

7. A visual timeline can be built by the readers to represent a tale. For example, incidents from the story can be drawn and hung on a clothesline in the sequence in which they occurred in the narrative.

8. The children can begin "versioning," developing their own story from a story they have heard or read. They can settle place, time, characters, details, mood, style, technique, displaying or binding strategies, designing a comparative study alone, in groups or as a class.

9. The children can magnify one small detail or incident in a story and prepare a close-up view of their vision of it. It may be a vignette only briefly mentioned, or a place not described, or an incident just referred to in the story.

10. A story quilt can be created, each contributor adding one patch to form the whole.

11. Masks can be created for characters in the story to wear while enacting or improvising from the story. Part of a group can respond to what others are saying or reading, using the masks and movement to interpret the story words.

12. Pictures can accompany the stories created by the children themselves as they stand on the shoulders of stories they have heard or read. One child may illustrate another's work, causing the two students to share details of interpretation so that the story and illustrations are a collaborative effort.

Celebrating Stories and Authors

In *Dear Mr. Henshaw*, Beverly Cleary mocks the reader/author interaction: the main character Leigh Botts writes to an author, Mr. Henshaw, for author information because of a school assignment. For four years, Leigh has handed in a book report on the same book, but now he contacts the author.

November 15

Dear Mr. Henshaw, At first I was pretty upset when I didn't get an answer to my letter in time for my report, but I worked it out OK. I read what it said about you on the back of Ways to Amuse a Dog and wrote real big on every other line so I filled up the paper. On the book it said you lived in Seattle, so I didn't know you had moved to Alaska although I should have guessed from Moose on Toast.

When your letter finally came I didn't want to read it to the class, because I didn't think Miss Martinez would like silly answers, like your real name is Messing A. Round, and you don't have kids because you don't raise goats. She said I had to read it. The class laughed and Miss Martinez smiled, but she didn't smile when I came to the part about your favorite animal was a purple monster who ate children who sent authors long lists of questions for reports instead of learning to use the library.

Your writing tips were OK. I could tell you meant what you said. Don't worry. When I write something, I won't send it to you. I understand how busy you are with your own books.

I hid the second page of your letter from Miss Martinez. That list of questions you sent for me to answer really made me mad. Nobody else's author put in a list of questions to be answered, and I don't think it's fair to make me do more work when I already wrote a report.

Anyway, thank you for answering my questions. Some kids didn't get any answers at all, which made them mad, and one girl almost cried, she was so afraid she would get a bad grade. One boy got a letter from an author who sounded real excited about getting a letter and wrote such a long answer the boy had to write a long report. He guessed nobody ever wrote to that author before, and he sure wouldn't again. About ten kids wrote to the same author, who wrote one answer to all of them. There was a big argument about who got to keep it until Miss Martinez took the letter to the office and duplicated it.

About those questions you sent me. I'm not going to answer them, and you can't make me. You're not my teacher.

Yours truly, Leigh Botts

P.S. When I asked you what the title of your next book was going to be, you said, Who knows? Did you mean that was the title or you don't know what the title will be? And do you really write books because you have read every book in the library and because writing beats mowing the lawn or shoveling snow?

Authors and illustrators are worthy of respect and must be treated carefully by teachers and schools. The sadness of the continued use of book reports in place of response activities points out the need we have as teachers for ways of working alongside professional storymakers in developing our children's story sense. Authors cannot handle all the requests for speaking or for answering letters, and we must help our children show consideration and understanding for these authors when they are fortunate enough to meet them in person or correspond through letters. Preparation is necessary for promoting the learning in these situations.

Meeting an author, illustrator, poet or storyteller is an exciting and motivating experience for children. With planning, such a meeting can become a story event, with invitations, promotion, organization, interviewing, discussion and follow-up activities all being organized with the children. They can use this "author awareness unit" to begin to understand the voice behind the words and /or pictures.

When children recognize professional authors as real people, they begin to see the writing of stories differently. They come to understand themselves as writers, and the authoring process is made accessible. The personal feelings that children develop from meeting authors promote further reading of selections by those authors, along with books on related themes. Stories are then seen as reflections of those who write them down, and children can see themselves as both readers and writers. We celebrate authors and storytellers and poets whenever and wherever possible. It is important that as much teaching potential as possible be gleaned from the experience of meeting authors. As organizer and resource person, the teacher can arrange the visit (check with your board to find out about funding — many boards have access to grants to cover the costs of bringing in authors), and then begin the preparation with the children — locating the writings and making them available, finding sources of biographical information, helping children to create a list of significant questions for an interview, planning with the children for invitations and thank-you letters, working with the writings, exploring the content, style and themes of the author, setting up displays that promote the author as writer for this celebration. Nothing is more demoralizing for an author than to be invited to a school where none of the children have read his or her work.

Designing an author unit involves the children examining a number of books written by the same author or author/illustrator. The children can read and listen to the author's work, then discuss, write and even learn more about the author's life and motivation for writing. Children are often curious about authors the class has read. They may have a working familiarity with the author and want to read other works by him or her. We can gather these and other books, audiotape and videotape references to the author and the work, newspaper and magazine clippings, and dramatized forms if possible.

With the children's help, we can make a display of the author's work and life in the classroom. Then, children can read this material on their own, as part of a small group, or with our help.

An author study seems to motivate the classroom community in a special way, and the children build special relationships with the story maker, which sends them into deeper and less familiar areas of literature and literacy. The story frame widens.

David Booth writes:

Visiting classrooms as an author sets up a very different context for my work in education. At these times I am perceived not as a teacher but as someone the children have already met virtually through the medium of my books, with expectations and ideas about who I will be and what I will represent. On two occasions, I introduced my books at the

Children's Bookstore to an audience of children from two to twelve years old. What intrigued me each time was the variety of their responses to the books, as we chatted after sharing them. These were, of course, children whose parents had brought them "to the books," and who were familiar with stories and authors.

Throughout my life I have been aware of paintings by the Group of Seven — on bank walls, in school halls and on postage stamps. There was never any doubt about the images of these trees of autumn, the shield of rock, the fields of winter; in them I recognized my country, bigger and bolder than I had known in my small town, but nonetheless a panorama of my Canadian dreams. Later, as I learned more about the artists and their work, these paintings came to represent my personal thoughts and feelings about this nation that sprawls across the top of the map. The Group captured the natural heart of Canada and wrapped me in its vision as if inside the flag.

The Canadian poems in the collection *Images of Nature* echo the paintings; the words filter through the artists' pine trees like a loon's call. Each time I read the poems and look at the pictures, I understand more deeply my country and my identity.

The children wrote memories of their own connections with nature, and the ones that follow capture a story moment as in a photograph.

Jamie's Nature Walk

I heard a bear.
It sounded like
Branches
Breaking
I didn't see it.
I only heard it.

Justin's Nature Walk

When I was walking
Up the hill
I found a deer
Horn.
I brought it home.
I'll probably never
Find one again.

Debbie's Nature Walk

Golden trees
Stand around me.
Green hills
Sleep beside me.
Swan-like clouds
Fly above me.
And my soul rings
Like a church bell.

Similarly, after I had read the book *The Dust Bowl* to the children, they wrote letters in role to Matthew, the boy in the story, about their lives after leaving the prairie farms. *The Dust Bowl* takes place fifty years after the great drought, when the prairies were once again as bone dry as they were during the 1930s.

The responses from the children touched me deeply, as I read their stories about my story, their constructs of what I had built with my words and the artist's images.

Dear Matthew

We moved to Bahamas. The palm trees are so nice by the surfside, the waves rolling in and splashing onto the hot sand of the beach. It's absolute paradise, sometimes it's so hot that you either have to spend the whole day in the water, or in the house.

The people sometimes harvest bananas at night. They are delicious and the wonderful aroma that rises from the market place, it's enough to make your mouth water.

Sincerely,
Uncle Ray

Dear Matthew,

When I moved I moved to Toronto and visited the C.N. Tower a few times. I miss the Prairies a lot and I want to come back but I can't. The Dust Bowl was scary that's why I don't want to come back. The Dust Bowl was the scariest thing that ever happened to me. I usually forget about it because I'm so busy with everything else. I read books about prairies to remember what it was like. I'm having fun. Bye!

Shannon

Authors in the Classroom

To help the children understand the challenge and process of publishing a story, a number of author/illustrators visited Larry Swartz' classroom and gave the children and the teacher insights into writing.

On one occasion Maryann Kovlaski visited our class and previewed her book *The Seven Chairs*. The students had been introduced to books illustrated by Maryann (*Jingle Bells, Take Me Out to the Ballgame, Doctor Knickerbocker, The Cake That Mack Ate, Grandmother's Secret, Mable Murple*). During her presentation, Maryann demonstrated her illustration technique on chart paper. She then invited the students practice drawings to accompany stories they had written.

The artist Warabe Aska also visited the classroom and explained how he works with the author David Day to match text to art. The class had been investigating his books and were intrigued with Aska's brightly coloured, surrealistic and detailed images (e.g., *Who Goes to the Park, Aska's Sea Creatures, Aska's Birds*). We also had a class trip to the local art gallery to see a showing of Aska's original paintings. I purchased postcards of scenes from *Aska's Animals* and gave one to give to each student. Accompanying each painting in the book, Aska has written a short legend to explain the birth of a number of animals such as the elephant, the zebra, and the swan. The children in the class used the poems and paintings to invent their own legends.

Canadian author Eric Walters, who has written a number of novels in the past decade (e.g., *Stars, Trapped in Ice*), discussed the process he goes through to write a story. For the novel *Tiger by the Tail*, which tells the story of an escaped tiger, Eric told the children that he went with his family to visit a friend who owned a tiger. Eric showed the class a video that he had taken of his visit and told them an anecdote about his son who was resting by the cage and was startled to see the tiger's paw on his shoulder. The scene was written into the novel.

Assessing Your Story Program

To develop a sense of story as central to your successful classroom program, the children need to experience all types of stories in a variety of forms, written, visual and oral, and feel involved in their storying experiences; they need opportunities to reflect upon their story experiences, to respond to what they have heard and read, and to share their responses.

As teacher, you need to represent a story model for your own students, valuing story in your own life, taking time to participate in storying activities personally and professionally, sharing your personal story experiences with students when opportunities arise. As you tell and read aloud stories to the whole class, or to a group, and as you read parts of books aloud, as well as other story resources (e.g., samples from your journals, letters you receive), you are adding to their story strengths. As well, as we have seen, guests can tell stories to your class, and tapes can be used.

By having the children engage in storying activities, such as retelling literary and life stories, retelling in role, writing from the story, engaging in research stimulated by the story, playing story games, and singing story songs, you are providing a culture of narrative building that will support and encourage the growth of the children's sense of story.

Your story program can affect curriculum learning in other areas, as you connect your storying activities to the contexts of the various content areas your class is investigating. Teaching about pioneers means sharing the stories of their lives.

The following outcomes represent some of the skills, concepts and strategies that we can employ when assessing a child's story development. A child who is learning through stories:

- is aware of a variety of stories in the classroom, in different curriculum areas, and at home (e.g., books, computers, magazines, television, family stories);
- listens to and appreciates stories told and read aloud (at home, at school, live, taped);
- responds emotionally to story (appreciates humour, sadness, etc.);
- retells favourite stories;
- shares stories during free time;
- tells stories outside of school;
- tells personal life stories from family and school;
- retells a story using words and phrases from the original;
- paraphrases a familiar story using her or his own words;
- connects, compares and contrasts stories read and told with personal life experience;
- considers extensions to stories that offer possibilities;
- asks questions about stories that reveal thoughtful interpretation;
- continues to develop a storehouse of stories;
- reads and tells stories in a variety of situations, individually, with a partner, in a small group, as a member of the classroom community;

- analyzes the strategies that were used in listening to or reading a story;
- reads aloud with phrasing and fluency;
- reads and tells stories independently and with confidence;
- can read intensively for an appropriate period of time;
- demonstrates sustained engagement with story;
- understands the main point of the story;
- predicts and confirms events in a story;
- relates emotionally to characters and events, ideas and concepts in the story;
- gives opinions about characters, their actions and beliefs;
- connects a story to similar stories;
- questions the information and the implications in a story to make the most meaning;
- understands stated and unstated events in the story;
- participates in discussions about stories, commenting on and listening to the ideas of other students;
- confirms and clarifies ideas by referring to the story, quoting relevant points when possible;
- changes opinions and beliefs, and modifies viewpoint;
- moves beyond summarizing a plot to significant responses to the whole story;
- compares the work of various authors and genres in stories;
- recognizes story patterns inherent in a genre;
- creates other forms of literature to demonstrate understanding and interpretation of a story;
- identifies and articulates the author's purpose for telling or writing a story;
- participates in shared story experiences;
- shows personal involvement when talking about stories in conferences and in journal writing;
- examines the ways in which authors present ideas in stories;
- reads and listens to stories critically and without bias;
- knows how different story structures work;
- reads a variety of fiction and non-fiction stories;
- identifies favourite genres, favourite authors;
- seeks meaning in a story different from personal experience;
- discusses elements of a story, including characters, settings, time period, plot, mood and structure, and is developing a knowledge of how the elements of a story work;
- recognizes how stories can contribute to personal development;
- appreciates how story reflects and extends knowledge of a culture;
- constructs meaning from a variety of stories, written for different purposes;
- chooses to read some stories aloud with effective interpretive skills;
- uses techniques and words drawm from a story when telling or writing;
- continues to develop as a self-motivated lifelong reader, writer and storyteller;
- values personal story achievements and those of others.

6

Choosing Stories for Sharing

Aunt Sue's Stories

Aunt Sue has a head full of stories.
Aunt Sue has a whole heart full of
stories.
Summer nights on the front porch
Aunt Sue cuddles a brown-faced child
to her bosom
And tells him stories.
Black slaves
Working in the hot sun,
And black slaves
Walking in the dewy night,
And black slaves
Singing sorrow songs on the banks of
the mighty river
Mingle themselves softly In the flow
of old Aunt Sue's voice,
Mingle themselves softly
In the dark shadows that cross and
recross
Aunt Sue's stories.
And the dark-faced child, listening,
Knows that Aunt Sue's stories are
real stories.
He knows that Aunt Sue
Never got her stories out of any book
at all,
But that they came
Right out of her own life.
And the dark-faced child is quiet
Of a summer night
Listening to Aunt Sue's stories.

Langston Hughes

We can demonstrate a myriad of activities to help children acquire story power, but our first strategy is for the adults in the classroom to select and share stories from all cultures for all children, to take the class places they could not go without us. If we can carry the stories to the children, they will welcome us, join us, and story alongside us; they will join the tribe. We choose a story to share with the children every time we meet them — daily or even more frequently — and we select stories that are suitable for the village square. We try to find stories that touch children of different ages, experiences, and abilities in different ways; the closeness of the class often helps everyone to find meaning in the story being shared aloud. We tend not to read to them what they read for themselves, or what they will read for themselves in the future. We choose a variety of story types and themes, stories that will affect them, surprise them, make them laugh, make them wonder, stories that model in their very being the strength of narrative. We enjoy sharing different versions of the same tale, perhaps a retelling with powerful illustrations, a story from an unfamiliar culture, a story from a time far from that of our students, a story that stands on the shoulders of other stories they may have met.

Where do we find all these stories that we need to build a storying community in the classroom, and which ones will appeal to the children? Story selection is highly personal; those we grow to love are not necessarily perfect examples of the art, nor are they always the ones we started out to find. The element of surprise is very much alive where story selection is concerned. The different ways in which each of us has come to stories will figure prominently in what we take into our classrooms to share. These personal encounters with stories are important indeed, often the story has found us, not vice versa.

Stories for Everyone

Lissa Paul, an authority in children's literature, feels that our understanding of gender is constantly being made and remade, supported by our encounters with stories. We learn how to "be" in response to the stories that we hear and participate in, and through the continual layering of these stories we learn how to participate in our culture. Thus the relationship between power and the stories we tell connects us to our sociocultural landscape in particular ways.

It may help to remember how we came to be as we are. This gendering may well be at the root of why we've inherited "girl books" and "boy books." Traditionally, boys' books often had boys as protagonists, were about adventures, fighting, sports and machines (cars, trains, planes and motorcycles). They might use pace and event at the expense of anything else, with narratives that were action-packed and lacking characterization and any sense of the inner life of the characters. However, girls' books were often about families, relationships, babysitting, horses or romance, and their writing might represent a greater awareness of a social and moral context for action. Of course, the success of Harry Potter seems to support an appeal to a range of readers, but the important point may be that they are indeed "readers."

Successful reading involves the ability to de-centre, to empathize, to enter the world of the text and identify with characters. Primary teachers often observe that boys do not get involved in roleplay or dressing up as readily as girls, and may indeed be discouraged from doing so. Empathetic reading is perhaps harder to achieve without a foundation in imaginative play, and some boys actively resist the kind of affective and involving experiences that fictional texts offer the reader.

Lissa Paul says that reflection and the capacity to explore one's own response to a text are fundamental aspects of developing as a mature reader. A reader must be able to focus on what happens to him or her and to register the ideas, associations, feelings and attitudes that he or she experiences while reading. This is the most important feature of "aesthetic" reading, and girls may be more accustomed to reflecting on their own feelings and responses in this kind of way, and to sharing these reflections with others.

Myra Barrs says that the teaching of reading necessarily involves the education of the emotions and of the whole person. The challenge for educators is how to make these forms of thinking and feeling more accessible to boys. We need to offer more intelligent solutions to the question of how to develop boys' and girls' reading. Full reading not only encourages us to examine our critical and aesthetic response to verbal texts, but also demands that we explore and re-examine our personal responses and attitudes relating what we read to our lives. We choose to read what we are becoming.

Author and teacher Bill Martin, Jr. describes his story journey in "A Memoir":

My first book reading came when I was twenty. In college. Yes, then even nonreaders were admitted to college or university if they could muster tuition fees. By this time in my life I was so skilled in masking my print blindness that most teachers thought I was lazy, unprepared, never suspecting that it was my ears, not my eyes, that opened Sesame. I have Miss Davis to thank. She tuned my ears to literate language, to the voice of the text. Not to the voice of Jack London, but to the voice of his story, "To Build a Fire." Not to the voice of Robert Louis Stevenson, but to the voice of Treasure Island. Not to the voice of James Whitcomb Riley, but to the voice of "Little Orphan Annie." Not to the voice of Daniel DeFoe, but to the voice of Robinson Crusoe. Now, years later, I have learned to search the page for the voice of the text in determining whether to devote reading time to an unfamiliar book. In this context, voice and comprehension are synonymous.

And we return to one of the resonances of this book — pay attention to the story, regard the images that fill your mind, trust the story to do its work. And what is a story?

Once we have discovered a story or the story has discovered us, it grows in our imaginations. Over time, comparisons are made with like tales; variants, especially if we are dealing with stories from the oral tradition, are found; familiar motifs are recognized; and story history and relatives come to be understood. Stories connect us to stories, patterns, and pathways; relationships criss and cross like skeins of wool on a loom and we are drawn into the pattern, fascinated, filled with the anticipation of new discoveries. The story chooses us.

Does the Teller Choose the Tale or Does the Tale Choose the Teller?

Among the questions teachers most often ask about children's books are:

• What sure-fire hits can you show us?
• What follow-up ideas can you give us?

The first question is tricky because in order to find "sure-fire" hits you must read a lot of books, talk to a lot of readers and take some risks. Not everyone likes the same thing. When it comes to follow-up ideas there is little doubt that what we do must help readers to be aware of what has taken place inside their heads as they listened or read and to pay attention to the responses which other individuals in the class have formulated.

Of course, knowing the children and their interests is absolutely essential in providing the material they need. In many instances, great patience and flexibility will be required, for we must, to a certain extent, go in the directions in which the children need to go. At the same time, the students' own publications must be integrated into the reading and sharing experiences of the classroom.

We choose stories to share that will provide an experience in storying rich enough, varied enough, that all our children will find something that they can and want to share with others. Our stories do not always

Something with a beginning, a middle, and an end, of course. But the lasting stories are more. If they are lacking that bit of "inner truth," then they are of no value. Without meaning, without metaphor, without reaching out to touch human emotion, a story is a poor thing: a few rags upon a stick masquerading as a living creature.

Jane Yolen
Favorite Folktales from Around the World

have happy endings, but they do offer hope and a future, even in coming to understand difficult situations such as loss or death. Cynicism and despair are not building blocks for children; story must leave a light shining somewhere in their eyes.

We may begin by introducing our story with a related tale or poem, or an activity that invites the children into the narrative, an anecdote from our own lives that touches on some event within the story to come, a role whereby we can set the mood or atmosphere, or draw on the experiences of the children who have prepared an introduction. One story read or told aloud can initiate the children into the next one, as stories build on one another. We like to have the stories we share available to the children for independent reading, along with related stories and media.

A Story Inventory

Folktales

My Uncle

One day my uncle was walking on a bridge. Suddenly he fell into the lake. Then he went home in wet clothes.

The next day he was sick. My grandma saw my uncle lying on the bed, so my grandma went to get medicine.

At night, my grandma dreamed that my uncle stepped on a skull when he fell in the lake. In the morning, my grandma knew that a person who had died in the lake didn't forgive him, so she went to the place where my uncle fell. She brought fruit and she put the fruit on a plate. Then she kneeled down and begged that person not to make my uncle sick.

Anh Vuong, Grade 6

No matter how ancient a story or folktale, it is not an archeological relic, but a living thing, subject to mutation. Tales are as likely to have grown as to have shrunk. They are glimpses into a particular time, recreating a culture's then current mores. They may have acquired more significance as they pass through time, or they may have been rubbed smooth.

Many such tales have been carried by immigrants to remote parts of the world. Thousands of stories have become a part of the repertoire of many tellers of tales. Once all tales were told and listened to by the unlettered, but beginning five or six thousand years ago, the scribe and his writings began to influence the tradition. The oral teller and his audience were of primary importance, however, and it is through them that these thousands of stories have spread so widely over thousands of miles, favourites both of children and of those who never grow old. This body of narrative tradition developed gradually, coming from many sources and taking many forms. Often the only versions we have are from literature. Certain authors have retold these tales in their own literary idioms and sometimes they have almost obliterated the original stories. Today's audience will never know how the ancient storytellers told them. The old stories were transmitted and changed by time and by the times, by the teller and by the listeners, by the country in which they arose and by the countries to which they were carried. The old tales were changed in the way culture itself changes. "As you follow a story through its changes, you follow the trade routes, the slave routes, the route of a conquering army or that of a restless people on the move. In the beginning, there was the oral tradition, but once writing was established, the written word worked its own magic on 'story,'" according to Jane Yolen.

The transcriber of the tale reshaped old materials but stayed within the limits of the traditional story. The literary folktale is modern and ancient at once, and it was born written. An example would be Joan Aiken's *The Moon 's Revenge*, in which she uses the patterns and motifs of long-ago tales: "There was once a boy named Sep who was the seventh son of a seventh son." Folktales are real, however. Taken all together, they offer examinations of human traits, a general explanation of life, a proof of humanity.

Jane Yolen says there are more than five hundred known versions of "Cinderella" for all ages and audiences, told and handed down for centuries.

Joseph Jacobs, quoted in Yolen's *Touch Magic*, once said about a Cinderella story he printed:

> It was an English version of an Italian adaptation of a Spanish translation of a Latin version of a Hebrew translation of an Arabic translation of an Indian original.

Each reteller brings to the telling something of his or her cultural orientation. Is the Chinese admiration for the tiny foot preserved in the Cinderella tale, or is it the seventeenth-century preoccupation with dressing for the ball? Did translations of Charles Perrault's version of the story of the slipper change the Cinderella story for all time, since "de vair" means of fur or ermine, and "de verre" means of glass.

In his psychological study, *The Witch Must Die: How Fairy Tales Shape Our Lives*, Sheldon Cashdan analyzes dozens of stories in terms of the seven deadly sins, and explains how children's empathy for a character like Snow White, who embodies Vanity, may be less important than their identification with the evil queen: "As children mature, 'kill thine enemy' needs to evolve into 'know thine enemy'…[They] need opportunities to become conversant with parts of themselves they are going to have to deal with for the rest of their lives."

There are now selections, collections, translations and illustrations for every age and experience in society. A single folktale that has inspired endless listening over the centuries motivates graphic artists such as Maurice Sendak and Michael Foreman to illustrate them.

Folktales are the bare bones of stories; they allow each individual to imagine and add details to the narrative. They say so much in so few words and they are easy to carry in the mind. Folk literature includes songs, ballads, plays, dances, jokes, superstitions, skipping rhymes, tongue twisters, charms, omens, riddles, games, verses, nursery rhymes, proverbs, fables, parables, tall tales, urban tales, fairy tales, anecdotes, epics, myths, legends and religious stories.

Stories of today are built on stories from the past. There is no shame in this borrowing. The author/illustrator Steven Kellogg has retold several larger-than-life legends that beg to be read aloud, alongside the wonderful illustrations that fill the page with visual stories. His picture books about Pecos Bill, Johnny Appleseed and Paul Bunyan strengthen our concept of tales to retell, of creating personal versions, and the colours, movement and humour of his paintings will fill children's minds with storying power.

Susan Jeffers builds a fairy tale theme of her own for all ages. Her breathtaking paintings draw special meanings from stories told over centuries, and children hear the words and see the pictures and begin to create their own enchanted versions of these text, and children can lose themselves in the crystal palaces, and find themselves in the classroom full of the memories of their journey, waiting to be shared. Look at her renderings of "The Snow Queen," "Cinderella" and "Thumbelina." All modern writers write about themselves, just as storytellers of old passed on stories that spoke to them and revealed images of themselves. A story can be read on many levels: a child reads it on one, an adult on another. The creators of modern literary tales for the young must recognize that the child takes the tale "to heart." The writer is the wise one to all children who read what is written: borrowed tales, transcribed tales, literary folktales. G.K. Chesterton, quoted by Nickolas Tucker in *The Child and the Book*, writes:

> If you really read the fairy tales, you will observe that one idea runs from one end of them to the other: the idea that peace and happiness can only exist on some condition, an idea that is the core of ethics, the core of the folktale.

Modern tales, borrowing characters and cadences from the folktale, reflect both the individual and society. Stories come out of and then go back into society, changing the shape of that society in turn, and modern mythmakers must not bear this burden lightly. In *Touch Magic*, Jane Yolen states that: "A story about a Prince would be historical. A story about a frog would be biological. But a story about a frog Prince is magical."

The storyteller is an artist, and selection is essential for art. There are thousands of characters, of details, of motifs. It takes great skill to choose. Ancient humans took in the world mainly by listening — the world was shaped by the oral traditions. The rememberers were the most attuned listeners: the poets, the storytellers, the shamans and the soothsayers. The carriers of the oral tradition were honoured. The early tales and stories from childhood came from asking questions similar to those that children ask, and the best answers of the shamans, the storytellers and the seers were collected in the oral channel until they reached print.

A tale well told forces a confrontation with the deepest kind of reality, giving the child a focus, the very taste of primary truth. Was the tale made centuries ago, or yesterday? The best of the stories touch the past and the present in all of us. Folktales, "the stories of the tribe," provide strong reading and listening materials for children. The context of "long ago" enables children to explore all the universal problems and concerns that have troubled humanity forever, but in a safe, non-threatening framework. The deeds of heroes, the schemes of tricksters, the lore of nations past, can all serve as settings for children's own development — family situations, societal difficulties, supernatural beliefs, natural phenomena.

Traditional literature — folk and fairy tale, myth and legend from all over the world and ranging from ancient civilizations to twentieth-century emerging nations — makes an excellent starting point for stories. Beautifully illustrated editions of myth, legend, and folk and fairy tale have flooded the market in recent years. One such outstanding example is Brock Cole's *The Giant's Toe*. This is a highly imaginative reworking of Jack and the Beanstalk and one destined to take its place alongside Raymond Briggs's wonderful parody, *Jim and the Beanstalk*. The fun of such retellings lies in the comparisons it invites. Other like sources and variations become the stuff of much speculation and detective work. Did Brock Cole get his idea about losing a toe in a vegetable patch from this old tale in Richard Chase's *American Folk Tales and Songs*?

The Big Toe

One time a little boy was hoein' taters. He was mad. He liked taters 'n beans for supper all right, but there wasn't any meat to put in the beans and he liked meat in his beans.

Well, he was hackin' with his hoe at a big weed when all-at-once somethin' scrambled under the dirt and went

"UR-R-R-R!"

— like it was hurt, and then it went off down under the ground like a big mole. The boy looked and there, lyin' in the dirt, was a big toe. He'd hacked off that somethin's big toe. He grabbed it up and ran for life! Tore open a few bean vines, knocked down several cornstalks, and jerked the button off the gate gettin' away from there. He made it to the house. Washed that big toe with a dipperful of water and put it in his overall pocket.

And when his Mommy was cookin' supper in the fireplace he eased up the potlid when she had her back turned and slipped that big toe in with the beans. So, when they got to the table and started eatin', that boy ate three big baits of beans — and in one of 'em his Mommy had scooped up that big toe. So he ate it.

Finally his Mommy got the dishes washed and the pots scoured and out the way, and his Daddy got in a load of firewood to cook breakfast, and the boy got in his pile of kindlin' wood, and then they were all sittin' around the fireplace with a lightwood slow burnin'. The boy's Mommy she sat on one side, and his Daddy sat on the other, and that boy he was sittin' cross-legged right in the middle of the hearthrock pokin' in the ashes with the poke-stick. And — all at once they heard somethin' way off "Wha wow woo wod." They sat right still, listenin'. Then they heard it again. It was comin' closer.

"Where mow wow woe!" The boy's Daddy jumped up and barred the door. They sat on sort of wonderin' and sort of scared — and then they heard it out in the road and comin' right that way! "Where's my big toe?" The boy's Mommy she jumped up and rolled under the bed, and his Daddy ran and crawled right in after her. They laid there a-shakin' and a-shiverin' so it rattled the bed-slats.

That little boy was so scared he couldn't move! Just sat there froze to the hearthrock. Then the gatechain rattled and he heard that thing crunchin' up the path. "Where's my big to-o-o-o-oe." Heard it climbin' up on the porch roof — scratched on up the shingles till it was on top of the house. "Where's my big to-o-o-o-o-oe.' Then it hollered right down the chimney. "Where's-my-big-TO-O-O-O-O-OE?" The little boy saw soot fallin', and he looked up, and there, sittin' on the smoke-shelf was a great-big-old hairy thing. Had big red eyes, big black bushy tail, big claws, and great long sharp snag-teeth. Says, "Where's my big-TO-O-O-O-OE? YOU GOT It."

And did Ian Serraillier write his poem from the memories of an old ballad that shares a similar theme?

The Visitor

A crumbling churchyard, the sea and the moon;
The waves had gouged out grave and bone;
A man was walking, late and alone...
He saw a skeleton on the ground;
A ring on a bony finger he found.

He ran home to his wife and gave her the ring.
"Oh where did you get it?"
He said not a thing.
"It's the loveliest ring in the world," she said,
As it glowed on her finger.
They slipped off to bed.
At midnight they woke.
In the dark outside,
"Give me my rind" a chill voice cried.

"What was that, William? What did it say?"
"Don't worry, my dear. It'll soon go away."

"I'm coming"
A skeleton opened the door.
"Give me my ring!"
It was crossing the floor.

"What was that, William? What did it say?"

"Don't worry, my dear. It'll soon go away."
"I'm reaching you now! I'm climbing the bed."
The wife pulled the sheet right over her head.
It was torn from her grasp and tossed in the air.
"I'll drag you out of bed by the hair!"
"What was that, William? What did it say?"
"Throw the ring through the window! THROW IT AWAY!"
She threw it.
The skeleton leapt from the sill,
Scooped up the ring and clattered downhill,
Fainter ... and fainter ... Then all was still.

Revisiting Folktales

We can incorporate folktales into the curriculum in a variety of ways:

- The children can retell or record stories they have heard from other relatives or friends. These stories can then be transcribed into print and published for the class.
- Take a survey of the kinds of tales the children want to hear about a specific culture: humorous stories, stories about growing into adulthood, stories about aging and death.
- Tell the children a story rather than read it. How does the story change? How do the children react?
- Read aloud a picture-book version of a folktale to the children. What interpretation has the artist placed on the story? What time and culture frames have been created? What values have been added or elaborated upon?
- Have the children design the setting for a tale you are going to read or tell; for example, are we shepherds on a hill, shivering in the cold? Are we in a clearing in a tropical rain forest in Africa?
- Children can bring in other forms of folklore, such as riddles, tongue twisters, recordings, skipping rhymes, chants.
- An integrated arts day may be held at the end of a folklore unit, including storytelling, folk-art display, puppet plays, songs, games, traditional foods.
- The children can watch a film of a folktale, discussing the filmmaker's interpretation of the story.

Picture Books

David Booth's experience:

I read the book *Owl Moon* by Jane Yolen to a class of student teachers to illustrate personal connections with literature, and their responses were so strong that I asked them to write them down. Subsequently, I made a class booklet for them which was distributed on the last day. I was so moved as they began to read them, for they stayed late into the afternoon, reading the stories of their friends, those students with whom they had worked for a year. All this from one picture book. The following is one of those reminiscences:

> Fishing is a big part of our family life, especially for the men. I come from a family with three other brothers. There is my older brother George who loves to fish so much that he has moved out to Vancouver Island, Campbell River, the "Salmon Capital" of the world, which they so proclaim. This is George's idea of Heaven on Earth. He can work and be his own boss with no one to bother him; he can fish in solitude in one of countless lakes and rivers; and he can smoke grass like they were cigarettes and no one thinks anything of it. My passion for fishing originates through him, because back in Toronto George is a legend when it comes to fishing. Particularly on the Danforth in Toronto's Greek community. You might say he is the Greek version of Red Fisher!

A long time ago, back in my country when I was 2 or 3 years old, my dad was a fisherman. One day my dad went out onto the ocean with my 8th oldest uncle and my 10th oldest uncle. I don't know what they were doing, but they were not fishing. My dad was in the ocean doing something when a water ghost tried to drown him. A water ghost is a spirit of someone who died in the water. My uncle helped my dad and he survived.

Thinh Phu, Grade 8

I remember as a child waking up in the early morning hours (sometimes 3:00 a.m., sometimes 4:00 a.m.) sneaking downstairs and watching George prepare with his friends for their trip. Just when he was about to leave I would pop my head out from where I was hiding and ask him if I could go. The response was almost always no! That would just kill me and I would go back upstairs to my room and cry myself back to sleep. Don't get me wrong, I did go on the occasional fishing trip, but those were like picnics with my parents, cousins and younger brothers. But to me, these didn't really count. George's trips seemed so mysterious and adventurous, and besides, he and his group would always bring back huge fish! I remember the day he brought back this incredible rainbow trout. Its colours were so bright and the fish was just so large that they had it mounted. For years this fish was a reminder to us of just how great a fisherman George was. It reminds me that fishing is the one thing that I have in common with him. We are both two different people with many opposing views, yet we (in fact all of us brothers) now have this one common love — fishing — that unites us and allows us to make conversation whenever we are all together for dinner.

Inside the Picture Book

The picture book presents an exciting opportunity for engaging children in contextual learning — not "talking about" but "being involved within." The words and pictures work together to synthesize a new creation, which appeals especially to today's visually oriented children. The age of the children seems almost irrelevant; the well-chosen picture book embodies those qualities of story and image that draw the child's own experience to the page and let the child see and hear new meanings, negotiating between the child's own world and that of the author/illustrator. If a group of children takes part in a shared reading/listening activity with a picture book, and if the children subsequently explore, exchange and clarify ideas and meanings through talk and movement, a learning situation develops that allows for maximum experiencing, and the children make sense not only of their individual responses to a book, but of each other's worlds. Picture books open up opportunities for discussion and therefore deepen understanding; the pictures draw the eye and the text catches the imagination.

In choosing picture books, we select stories with strong narratives. Folktales or contemporary stories with folk quality help the children travel to another time — an imagined past, an analogous present, an anticipated future. The words can offer powerful language input for the child, story vocabulary, new and varied syntactic patterns, strong contextual clues for exploring meaning, characters who struggle with life's problems — sometimes symbolic, sometimes very real. With such stories, the children are engaged in experiencing language more complex than their own.

Whether the books are labeled picture books or illustrated books, their pictures provide visual input for the child, even for the non-reader. Picture books run the gamut of styles and techniques — watercolours, woodcuts, lithography, photography and collage; they illuminate the text; they extend the words into possibilities of meaning; they shock the reader/listener with new interpretations, lifting the child's own experience into different conceptual realms. The old is made new; the new is made relevant; the negotiation for meaning continues. The picture book is a demanding medium, especially for older readers. As the artist has brought a personal reality to the words, so children can interpret the meanings of the art individually and collectively. In most cases, the pictures do not hamper or imprison creative thought; rather, they give structure to energy, lifting the children's ideas, offering patterns for beginnings, suggestions for bouncing against. They present shape, line, colour and proportions as hooks for contrast and comparison. The very difference in the child's view of what is read, heard and then seen enables the child to distinguish that difference for what it is, the stimulus for looking at one's own particular universe with new eyes. Children can create their pictures in time and space, just as a new author/illustrator may take the story and present an entirely new concept through graphic design.

There are picture books of every type that will meet the needs of particular children. Like some films, a picture book can be a pleasure for an audience spanning a wide age range. Just as films such as *The Lion King* and *The Little Mermaid* can be viewed by the whole family, children in the middle years can share in the delight of the picture book and experience stories, memoirs, concepts and dreams as interpreted by authors and artists using photographs, collage, etches, oils, watercolour and other media. The text within a picture book must be written concisely and with the art in mind, so that children gain from it a particular and effective communication package. Since picture books were designed to be read aloud, children can experience the literature through both the ear and the eye, and perhaps be touched by the emotional quality inherent in this art form.

The picture book speaks to most children; it speaks to the child in all of us. Its origins are in cave paintings, in tapestries, in the stories of stained-glass windows. We can help the children see those paintings with stronger eyes and critical minds.

Story Poems

Some poems spin tales and report on people, places and events, all done with the ear and the eye of the artist. Poets have stories to tell. Long before most people could read or write, stories and tales were remembered through ballads and songs. Longer story poems used to be more popular than they seem to be today. The rhyme and the rhythm of the poetic form helped to shape the story, and offered help in remembering it. For these reasons, story poems are often effective for choral speaking and dramatizing. Some story poems are built around plot; others have stories hidden beneath the lines. Sometimes the story lies only in the mind of the poet or the reader/listener.

Today, poetry anthologies and songbooks abound, and teachers can choose from all types to satisfy their particular interests. Some of these books are beautifully illustrated, while others depend upon the strength of the imagination. Authors and song-writers select past favorites (often adapting or rewriting them), use well-known patterns on which to build new ideas, and create wonderful new sounds and images to delight children through the ear. The language structures and vocabulary that are embedded in poem and song offer a hoard of word power for future meaning making with print. Beginning with the success of Shel Silverstein, there has been an explosion of poetry for children. The humour, pathos and wonder that can be created in a few words seem to represent perfectly the needs of many youngsters. Successful poets know both the interests and the nature of children, and they evoke significant and emotional responses that may surprise adults. Freed from the rhythms and rhymes of jingles and verses, the writers explore all types and formats of poetry, and the children are able to join the word play because there is intellectual and emotional satisfaction in it. Talking about the images we see, listening to the musical sounds we hear and retaining some idea of what we think the story is telling us should be central to our work with storytelling in the classroom. If this is so, the problems of bringing story poems to life will turn into a real adventure. At the same time, our memories of the stories we have worked with will have been enriched by the involvement of our community of classroom storytellers.

A Story Collage

The following demonstrates how one class probed deeper into Judith Nicholls's "Moses ... A sequence."

Before introducing the poem, the teacher read from the Old Testament the story of Moses and the exodus from Egypt. She asked the children to be aware of any five things that made a pattern. At the conclusion of the reading, the children made lists of patterns they had discovered. For example, some made lists of magical transformations (e.g., burning bush, staff to serpent, water to blood), others made lists of water imagery. The children were then asked to explain the "big idea" behind their patterns.

Using an overhead projector, the teacher introduced the five poems that comprise "Moses . . . A sequence." After the children had opportunities to read the poems silently and out loud, they attempted to figure out the big idea behind Nicholls's pattern. They settled on groups of speakers, each telling an aspect of the Moses story from unique points of view. To test their ideas, each poem was assigned to a group whose task was to bring to life the voice of the speaker, and to convey in the oral reading both the intended audience and the purpose for telling the story. Here is the first poem in the sequence:

Searcher

Princess, what are you dreaming, down among the moist rushes? Soft pleated linen, beaded bracelets, purple grapes and Pharaoh's finest wines await you at the palace yet you follow a wavering baby's cry.

The group working with this selection settled on the voices of ladies-in-waiting, gossiping among themselves in the bulrushes as they observed Pharaoh's daughter following the cries of the baby Moses. Hushed voices and mocking tones were employed to put this across.

Interpretation of the other pieces ranged from work songs of labourers told in call-and-response fashion to games played by children to a cast rehearsal of a play celebrating the crossing of the Red Sea by descendants of those ancient Israelites. For these children, the saga of Israel became just that, and by approaching story in this way, the children were learning that storytelling is as much about how the story is shaped as it is about what happened to whom and why.

The more they talked about it, thought about it and revisited it, the greater became their awareness of the incredible energy and power that stories possess.

Novels

For many children, novels provide road maps for the difficulties of contemporary life, and they identify and live through the exploits of the fictitious characters they read about. Through themes, adults can help children deal with specific concerns via a range of novels that meet their wants and needs. Often, the teacher can work with novels that the children have read as a class, that a group has read, different novels on a theme, or a novel that has been read aloud to the class over a period of time. As well, the teacher can set up storying activities that prepare a class for a novel, or read the novel alongside the class. A novel contains a wealth of stories inside, and will promote through response dozens of others.

Children gain reading power through in-depth experiences with novels. Authors seem to understand the needs of children, and there are many fine books from which to choose. Children enjoy reading several books by a favoured author, or a series of books about a familiar set of characters. Common themes link the most widely read books — humour, school friends, mystery, fantasy — and children should be given as many opportunities as possible for reading independently. Boys and girls may prefer different types of books, and yet there are fine novels that, if brought to their attention, will fill their interest needs and present non-sexist portrayals.

For generations, children have enjoyed a body of novels that seem never to age or date. Because of the universal truths that hold constant, children can read or listen to books that portray a different life from their own, in custom, place, time or circumstance. For some children, these differences make the reading difficult, and the stories may have to be read to them. Novels for young adolescents allow readers to engage in a dialogue with an author on a wide range of topics at a deep, emotional level. The themes of these novels reflect the development of young adolescents, their concern about their place in the adult world, ecology, peace, the future and the past. As adults, we must understand the need these young readers have to understand life's problems, and accept that the portrayal and careful and artful examination of issues within the novel form will help consolidate and clarify their values and beliefs.

A Parcel of Patterns

One teacher approached a very challenging novel with a group of sixteen-year-olds. *A Parcel of Patterns* by Jill Paton Walsh deals with the struggles of the residents of the English village of Eyam to fight the Black Plague during the latter half of the 1600s. It is a tale of collective heroism as the residents, hoping to contain the ravages of the plague, vow to remain in their own village no matter what. The work resonates with echoes of the struggle to contain the AIDs virus that threatens our own age.

The novel itself sets up some interesting challenges for the reader. First, there are no distinct chapter divisions. The work proceeds through patterns of stories weaving in and among themselves. There is, for example, the story of the village, its time and its character. There is the story of Mall Percival, the central narrator. There is the story of two parsons. There is the story of beliefs, customs and rituals of the time. There is the story of the rich and the poor, and there is the story about storytelling, for in their attempts to fight the plague, the villagers lean heavily on three kinds of stories. First, the word of God as explained to them by their parsons; second, the words of their ancestors as contained in their folk sayings and rituals; and third, the stories that they make and tell each other about the plague as they see it.

Added to this is the manner of speaking that characterized Puritans living at the time. A terrific challenge and well worth it, every bit.

The teacher in this case realized that here was a book that would require a good portion of time building up high levels of anticipation. In order to waste no time capturing his students' attention, he decided to use a technique that filmmakers have employed for years to whet interest. He would first "preview" the work by plunging his students right into the middle of it. The reading commenced at the following point in the text:

> Now word was out it was the Plague we had; such secrets do not keep for long. Folk took fright at it. On the morrow of the day when my mother had been offended at Parson Momphesson's counsel, we were awoken from our beds by such a clattering and to-do in the street as we had seldom heard; and going to the casements and brushing off the breath-dew upon the glass, we saw three empty carts going up the town. As we took breakfast there came a neighbour to tell us that they were gone up to Sheldon's Farm; and ere we were done eating the carts came down again, laden high with chests and chairs and bundles, and the baby strapped on the top of the curtain-bale, crying loud, and manservants and maidservants carrying, or driving cows, and the little boy Sheldon leading the goat, and Mistress Sheldon bearing in her arms a loudly quacking hamper of withy-weave. Even the ducks from the pond were going away!
>
> As you may well suppose, this noise and spectacle brought families staring into every doorway in the road; and they had their fill of it too, for at the tail of the procession came Mistress Agnes Sheldon, Farmer Shel-

don's spinster sister, a deal older than he and a thorn in his flesh daily, as all the world well knew. And as she walked she railed upon him.

"Going to Hazleford, indeed," she cried. "Since when was Hazleford grand enough for Sheldons, may I ask?" "Thou hadst best hold thy tongue, and come too, sister," said Farmer Sheldon.

"Fie upon you, brother, for a cowardly man! What will the neighbours think!" cried she. And, lest we didn't think what she supposed, she continued, "I'll tell thee — they'll wonder what evil deed is on thy conscience, brother, that thou art afraid of the Lord's vengeance! An honest man fears not the Plague, but trusts in God! Oh, thou shameful fellow, thou . . ."

"Go to, sister, go to," he said, hanging down his head. And by now half the town was trotting along behind the trundling carts, and the shouting woman, all ears and smiles. My mother and I went along with all the rest; my father had more dignity, but he missed the best of it.

Beside the churchyard gate she baited him at last to stand at bay. "There is a foul contagion here," he said. "And we are going to a place of clean airs and safety until it has passed. And, sister, I implore thee for thy own health to come with us..."

He hath another farm at Hazleford," she told the eager crowd, "which ever till now my lady his wife thought not fit for her — though she hath tried very hard to make me dwell in it — and now, lo! Suddenly it is good enough and more. Bad conscience, bad conscience, say I! That baggage his wife hath cause to fear the Lord's displeasure, and dare not say that the righteous shall fear no ill, nor should..."

The students read the excerpt silently. They were encouraged to jot down any thoughts, reactions or questions that occurred to them. Next, in pairs, each told the other what they had visualized as the incident unfolded.

The whole class came together to share their images. Some students had very sharp pictures in their minds. "I saw the baby's head bobbing on top of the furniture piled on the cart." Others had less clear images, but had a feeling of the moment, like a sort of hazy pencil sketch or line drawing. Still others reported being aware of their own physical relationship to the scenes they witnessed. "I was inside a house, peeking out through an opening in the curtains." When they had nearly exhausted their thoughts, the teacher directed the students to reread the excerpt, paying particular attention to moments of conflict.

The students formed small groups after the reading and, acting on the teacher's instructions, chose one conflict to reproduce for readers' theatre. Because this excerpt dealt with a crowd, the students were encouraged to build some improvisation in and around the segments to be read. For most groups, this translated into crowd reaction to the reader's words. Each group took turns reading its prepared scene to at least one other group.

The whole class reconvened, and the teacher discussed with the students the difficult decision Farmer Sheldon had taken. The children were then asked to anticipate additional decisions that they thought the characters in the novel might face. At the conclusion of this discussion, each student was asked to write a diary entry in the role of a villager who described one of these difficult decisions.

Finally, the class divided into groups of five. One member of each group was to be an artist, the others his or her models. The groups were asked to create a "living painting" that informed the class about the lives of ordinary people living in Eyam during the plague.

The artists and their subjects used their diary entries for their ideas, then tableaux were shaped under each artist's direction. The session concluded with the viewing of each "living painting" as the artist explained to the viewers the artistic decisions that had been made in putting across the ideas. Copies of the novel were now distributed to the eager hands stretched out in excitement and anticipation.

Non-fiction Books

History is best told through the stories of others. Children — and adults — need to see the common thread that binds us to those who have come before, to make a personal connection to what has come before. To tell stories about the past is to understand our selves in relationship to others. In *Actual Minds, Possible Worlds*, Jerome Bruner writes:

> Each of the ways of knowing…has operating principles of its own and its own criteria of well-formedness. They differ radically in their procedures for verification. A good story and a well-formed argument are different natural kinds…The epistemological question….[is] how to know truth…the broader question…[is] how we come to endow experience with meaning.

Until recently, good information books at appropriate reading levels were scarce. Children could appreciate the photographs, pictures and diagrams in a given book, but adults were needed to interpret the writing. Today, authors for children are realizing that there is a growing audience for information presented aesthetically and effectively in books geared to children's abilities and interests. Adults must be wary of books that purport to present facts but have no appeal or artistic merit, no story. Everything a child reads contributes to his or her picture of what a book can offer, and information books must be no exception.

Several years ago, the film critic Pauline Kael, when asked what kinds of film she preferred, declared that she only wanted to see documentaries that told a great story.

In working with a story drawn from documents from the 12th century in England, one class explored its origins through drama:

> A merman was caught at Orford in Suffolk during the reign of Henry II (1154-1189). He was imprisoned in the newly-built castle, did not recognize the Cross, did not talk despite torture, returned voluntarily into captivity having eluded three rows of nets, and then disappeared never to be seen again. That's what the chronicler Ralph of Coggeshall says in his "Chronicon Anglicanum."

> Kevin Crossley-Holland,
> "The Wildman"

In small groups, round robin fashion, the children pretended the incident had been passed on in family stories. They recalled what they knew from their families about this "handed-down" incident. The story-telling was in the third person. The groups created three tableaux in sequence which explained the origins of the Wildman.

In pairs, the children improvised stories about the Wildman's appearance in the village. They also developed movement stories, which depicted a meeting between a villager and the Wildman. These stories were developed into a movement play entitled *The Encounter*.

The children visited the Wildman's world beneath the sea through Walt Whitman's poem, "The World below the Brine." They read it together chorally, then created the movement sequences that portrayed the passage from ocean depths to eventual emergence on land.

Kevin Crossley-Holland's retelling of *The Wildman* proved to be a very exciting discovery, for in many instances there were similarities between the children's retellings and that of a respected author.

7

Final Thoughts

Did the story happen to me?
Did I borrow the story?
Should I have borrowed the story?
Can I put myself in your story? (Will you know my presence there?)
Is it my story when you write it?
Is it my story if I read yours aloud?
Can two people own a story?
Can anyone own a story?
Are there stories I shouldn't hear?
Are there stories I shouldn't tell?
Did I dream my story?
Did you dream the same one?
Will you read me a story?
Will you tell me a story?
If you do, is the story yours?
Does it become mine in the sharing?
If I tell the story, whose words should I use?
Will you listen to my story?
Will you join in the telling?
Shall we sing the story?
Shall we paint the story?
Shall we dance the story?
Can you find another story like this one?
Where did you find it?
May I have it?
May I tell it?
Am I the story?

The magic of story is that as we become absorbed in a passionate, creative and sometimes fearful process, the story changes as we change, as we listen to ourselves, becoming at once the teller and the told. We relisten, as Jack Maguire writes in *The Power of Personal Storytelling*, to "what our deep memories and creative voices have to say to us once we've silenced our mind's surface chatter." We know that we will be shaped by the story, as will the children. And in the process, we, and they, may learn how story works. Of course, in the end, when we leave this world behind, all that truly remain are the stories.

Aunty Sheila

I never really knew my Aunty Sheila, I only heard stories about her. I would like to share my story with you about her life.

My dad grew up in a large family. (He had 8 brothers and 4 sisters.) The oldest child was my Aunty Sheila. They all lived in a place called Whim. Now in Guyana there is a tradition for the oldest girl to take care of her brothers and sisters, and Aunty Sheila took on that role. Although she had to cook and clean, she still had time to go to school and to parties. My dad says that Aunty Sheila was very pretty, and when it was time for her to get married she had many offers.

She chose the one person she thought was the best and got married. Although she was married Aunty Sheila still worked hard. Aunty Sheila had 8 children (6 boys and 2 girls) and she loved them very much and tried her best to take care of them. My dad who was the closest to my Aunty Sheila, went to visit her every day when she got married.

After having 8 children, Aunty Sheila was pregnant again. But the baby died at birth, which later resulted in Aunty Sheila having a hemorrhage. Each day, Aunty Sheila became sicker and sicker and she knew deep down that she was going to die. My father tried his best to take care of her but it was no use. She continued to get sicker and sicker. Her children stayed at my grandmother's house while she was sick, and my father said that she couldn't stop worrying about them and how they would grow up and get by in life.

One day when my father went to visit her, he found her really sick. He knew it was too late for him to take her to the hospital. His heart was crushed to see her lying there helpless. She too, knew that this was her time to die and she wouldn't stop talking about her children and what would become of them. So my father promised that he would take care of the children and that they would stay with him.

As time passed, my dad couldn't help but burst into tears while holding on tightly to her hand. He felt no life in her. My aunt's husband was not there when she died and he died the following year of an accident while working in the rice fields. The children became orphans, but my dad kept his promise and brought them to Canada.

Christine Katryan, Grade 8

Stories are invitations to joy, and we cannot be grateful enough for our time spent experiencing and exploring stories with young people. It has been a constant quest to find the most appropriate story for a group at a given moment, and a continuing adventure developing significant response activities that would lead into the story and into the lives of the children, both at once.

The stories of children live beside the stories of their families, alongside the stories of their friends, and in the shadows of the stories authored and transcribed by others. We cannot value one over the other. Each and all are part of the storying world that we inhabit from birth to death.

The place called school represents a fine locus for working with stories, where we can discover and share and talk about and build stories together, bonds of narrative that link us inextricably. For many children, the stories in print that we bring to them may have to do for all their lives. Others will continue to fill their story bags until they need steamer trunks to contain them. It takes so many stories to become human — some spill out, some are forgotten, others only remain as bits and pieces. But no matter. In the sifting and the sorting of our story lives, we will all the time be developing our story sense, and as we retell one from memory, the remnants of others will haunt the present one and colour it with hues unimagined. In the museums of our minds, the stories will touch each other, rub against each other, alter shape and substance, mix metaphor and symbol, become the ordinary and the fabulous. We celebrate the children who teach us anew every time we story with them.

We celebrate the teachers who plunge into story pools with children. We celebrate the authors and illustrators who write down, retell, invent and illuminate stories from and for all people.

But most of all, we sing the praises of the story — that most simple and complex creation of all the arts, resonating from caves and echoing from the moons of distant planets. We are all part of the story tapestries of our tribes, our threads woven into yours, each tale embroidered with the strands of others, for all time.

As Gregory Bateson wrote in *Mind and Nature*:

A man wanted to know about mind, not in nature, but in his private large computer. He asked it (no doubt in his best Fortran), "Do you compute that you will ever think like a human being?" The machine then set to work to analyze its own computational habits. Finally, the machine printed its answer on a piece of paper, as such machines do. The man ran to get the answer and found, neatly typed, the words:

That reminds me of a story.

References

Abrahams, Roger. 1985. "Why Hens Are Afraid of Owls," in *African American Folk Tales*. New York: Pantheon.

Agard, John. 1986. *Say It Again, Granny!* London: Bodley Head.

Aiken, Joan. 1987. "On Imagination" in *Innocence and Experience*, edited by Barbara Harrison and Gregory Maguire. New York: Lothrop, Lee and Shepard.

Allison, C. 1987. *I'll Tell You A Story, I'll Sing You A Song: A Parents' Guide to the Fairy Tales, Fables, Songs, and Rhymes of Childhood*. New York: Delacorte.

Anderson, Andy. 1999. "Running with the Story," in *Orbit*, Volume 30, Number 3.

Andrews, J., and K. Reczuch. 1990. *The Auction*. Toronto: Groundwood.

Anno, Mitsumasa. 1978. *Anno's Journey*. New York: Philomel.

Ashely, L.F. 1978. "Aspects of Animal Tales," in *English Quarterly*, Volume XI, Number 3, Fall 1978.

Ayers, W.C., et al, eds. 1998. *A Light in Dark Times: Maxine Greene and the Unfinished Conversation*. New York: Teachers College Press.

Barrs, Myra. 2000. "Gendered Literacy," in *Language Arts*, Vol. 77, No. 4, March.

Barrs, Myra, and Sue Pigeon. 1998. *Boys and Reading*. London: Centre for Language and Primary Education.

Barton, Bob. 1999. "The Art of Storytelling," in *Orbit*, Volume 30, Number 3.

Barton, Bob. 2000. *Telling Stories Your Way*. Markham: Pembroke.

Barton, Bob, and David Booth. 1990. *Stories in the Classroom: Storytelling, Reading Aloud and Roleplaying with Children*. Markham: Pembroke.

Bateson, Gregory. 1988. "That Reminds Me of a Story," in *Mind and Nature*. New York: Bantam.

Bateson, M.C. 1980. *Composing a Life: Life as a Work in Progress: The Improvisations of Five Extraordinary Women*. New York: Penguin.

Bennett, J. 1979. *Learning to Read with Picture Books*. Lockwood: Thimble Press.

Berg, L. 1977. *Reading and Loving*. London: Routledge and Kegan Paul.

Bernheimer, K., ed. 1998. *Mirror, Mirror on the Wall: Women Writers Explore Their Favorite Fairy Tales*. New York: Doubleday.

Bettelheim, B. 1975. *The Uses of Enchantment: The Meaning and Importance of Fairy Tales*. New York: Vintage Books.

Bierhorst, John. 1987. *Doctor Coyote*. Toronto: Macmillan.

Bishop, R. 1992. *Multicultural Literature for Children: Making Informed Choices. Teaching Multi-cultural Literature in Grades K-8.* Norwood, MA: Christopher-Gordon.

Bissex, Glenda. 1985. *GNYS AT WRK: A Child Learns to Write and Read.* Cambridge: Harvard University Press.

Blos, Joan. 1985. *Brothers of the Heart.* New York: Scribner.

Bodger, J. 1999. *How the Heather Looks.* Toronto: McCelland and Stewart.

Bomer, R. 1995. *Time for Meaning: Crafting Literate Lives in Middle & High School.* Portsmouth: Heinemann.

Booth, David. 1972. "Owl Trouble," in *Colours.* Toronto: Longman.

Booth, David. 1984. *Drama in the Formative Years.* Ontario Ministry of Education.

Booth, David. 1992. *Stories to Read Aloud.* Markham: Pembroke.

Booth, David. 1994. *Story Drama: Reading, Writing and Role-playing across the Curriculum.* Markham: Pembroke.

Booth, David, ed. 1995. *Images of Nature.* Toronto: Kids Can Press.

Booth, David, and Bill Moore. 1988. *Poems Please! Sharing Poetry with Children.* Markham: Pembroke.

Booth, David, and K. Reczuch. 1996. *The Dust Bowl.* Toronto: Kids Can Press.

Bradford, A., et al. 1999. "Summertime and the Reading is Easy," in *Currents in Literacy*, Volume 2, Number 2.

Britton, J. 1979. *Language and Learning.* London: Penguin.

Browne, Anthony. 1983. *Gorilla.* London: Julia MacRae Books.

Browne, Anthony. 1986. *Piggybook.* New York: Knopf.

Bryce, Helen, ed. 1999. *Family Stories from Lord Dufferin P.S.* Toronto: Toronto District School Board.

Burningham, J. 1974. *The Rabbit.* London: Random House.

Burningham, J. 1984. *Granpa.* London: Crown Publishers.

Butler, Dorothy. 1975. *Cushla and Her Books.* Boston: Horn Book.

Calkins, L.M. 1986. *The Art of Teaching Writing.* Portsmouth, NH: Heinemann.

Calkins, L.M. 1991. *Living between the Lines.* Portsmouth, NH: Heinemann, 1991.

Canfield, J., et al. 1996. *A Cup of Chicken Soup for the Soul.* Deerfield Beach: Health Communications Inc.

Carrick, Carol. 1986. *What Happened to Patrick's Dinosaurs.* New York: Clarion Books.

Carrick, Donald. 1982. *Harald and the Giant Knight.* New York: Clarion Books.

Cashdan, Sheldon. 1999. *The Witch Must Die: How Fairy Tales Shape Our Lives.* New York: Basic.

Caulfield, Judy. 1999. "The Storytelling Club," in *Orbit*, Volume 30, Number 3.

Causely, Charles. 1986. "Charity Chadder," in *Early in the Morning*. London: Viking Kestrel.

Chambers, Aidan. 1985. *Booktalk*. London: Bodley Head.

Chase, Richard. 1956. "The Big Toe," in *American Folk Tales and Songs*. New York: Signet Key Books.

Chukovsky, K. 1963. *From Two to Five*. Berkeley: University of California Press.

Clandinin, D.J., and M.F. Connelly. 1995. *Teachers' Professional Knowledge Landscapes*. New York: Teachers College Press.

Cleary, Beverly. 1983. *Dear Mr. Henshaw*. New York: Dell.

Cole, Brock. 1986. *The Giant's Toe*. New York: Farrar, Straus, Giroux.

Coles, Robert. 1989. *The Call of Stories: Teaching and the Moral Imagination*. Boston: Houghton Mifflin.

Coles, Robert. 1997. *The Moral Intelligence of Children*. New York: Random House.

Connelly, F.M., and D.J. Clandinin. 1988. *Teachers as Curriculum Planners: Narratives of Experience*. Toronto: OISE Press.

Connelly, F.M., and D.J. Clandinin. 1998. *Storied Identities: Storied Landscapes*. New York: Teachers College Press.

Connelly, F.M., and D.J. Clandinin. 1999. *Narrative Inquiry: Experience and Story in Qualitative Research*. San Francisco: Jossey-Bass.

Cormier, Robert. 1977. *I Am the Cheese*. New York: Dell.

Cox, S., & Galda, L. 1990. "Multicultural Literature: Mirrors and Windows on a Global Community," in *The Reading Teacher*, April, 1990.

Crago, H., and M. Crago. 1983. *Prelude to Literacy*. Carbondale: Southern Illinois University Press.

Crites, S. 1971. "The Narrative Quality of Experience," in *Journal of the American Academy of Religion*, 30 (3).

Crossley-Holland, Kevin. 1999. *The Old Stories*. London: Orion.

Davidson, D.M., et al. 1994. *Write from the Start*. Boston: Heinle & Heinle.

Davis, D. 1993. *Telling Your Own Stories: For Family and Classroom Storytelling, Public Speaking, and Personal Journaling*. Little Rock: August House.

DeBono, Edward. 1972. *Children Solve Problems*. Harmondsworth: Penguin.

De Regniers, Beatrice Schenk. 1976. *Little Sister and the Month of Brothers*. New York: Clarion Books.

De Roin, Nancy, ed. 1975. *Jataka Tales: Fables from the Buddha*. New York: Dell.

DeVos, Gail and Ann E. Altman. 1999. *New Tales for Old*. Libraries Unlimited.

Dewey, J. 1938. *Experience and Education*. New York: Collier Books.

Drake, Susan M. 1996. "Towards a New Story in Education," in *Orbit*, Volume 27, Number 1.

Drake, Susan M. 1998. *Creating Integrated Curriculum*. Thousand Oaks, CA: Corwin.

Duthie, Christine. 1996. *True Stories*. Portland, ME: Stenhouse.

Dyson, Anne Haas, ed. 1989. *Collaboration Through Writing and Reading*. Urbana, IL: National Council of Teachers of English.

Dyson, Anne Haas, and Celia Genishi, eds. 1994. *The Need for Story*. Urbana, IL: National Council of Teachers of English.

Edinger, M., et al. 1998. *Far Away and Long Ago: Young Historians in the Classroom*. Portland, ME: Stenhouse.

Edwards, Richard. 1987. *The Word Party*. Harmondsworth: Puffin.

Egan, Kieran. 1987. *Teaching as Story Telling*. London, ON: Althouse Press.

Engel, S. 1995. *The Stories Children Tell: Making Sense of the Narratives of Childhood*. New York: W.H. Freeman & Co.

Feuerverger, G. 1994. "A Multicultural Literacy Intervention for Minority Language Students," in *Language and Education*, 8(3).

Fields, Julia. 1988. *The Green Lion of Zion Street*. New York: Margaret K. McElderry Books.

Florian, D. 1998. *Insectlopedia*. San Diego: Harcourt Brace.

Fox, Carol. 1993. *At the Very Edge of the Forest*. New York: Cassell.

Fox, Mem, and T. Denton. 1989. *Night Noises*. San Diego: Harcourt Brace Jovanovich.

Fraser, A., ed. 1992. *The Pleasure of Reading*. Toronto: Knopf.

Fry, Donald. 1985. *Children Talk about Books: Seeing Themselves as Readers*. Milton Keynes: Open University Press.

Fulford, Robert. 1999. *The Triumph of Narrative*. Toronto: Anansi.

Fullan, M., et al. 1998. *The Rise and Stall of Teacher Education Reform*. Washington: American Association of Colleges for Teacher Education.

Garfield, Leon. 1982. *King Nimrod's Tower*. New York: Lothrop, Lee and Shepard.

Gass, W. H. 1999. "In Defense of the Book: On the Enduring Pleasures of Paper, Type, Page, and Ink," in *Harper's*, November 1999.

Gillard, M. 1996. *Storyteller, Storyteacher: Discovering the Power of Storytelling for Teaching and Living*. Portland, ME: Stenhouse.

Godina, H. 1996. "The Canonical Debate: Implementing Multicultural Literature and Perspectives," in *Journal of Adolescent and Adult Literacy*, April 1996.

Grainger, T. 1992. *Traditional Storytelling in the Primary Classroom*. London: Scholastic.

Granahan, Louise. 1999. "Window, Miracle and Vehicle: Multicultural Children's Literature," in *Orbit*, Volume 30, Number 3.

Graves, D.H. 1989. *Investigating Nonfiction*. Portsmouth, NH: Heinemann.

Green, J. 1999. *The Ultimate Guide to Classroom Publishing*. Markham: Pembroke.

Greene, M. 1995. *Releasing the Imagination: Essay on Education, the Arts, and Social Change*. San Francisco: Jossey-Bass.

Grifalconi, Ann. 1986. *The Village of Round and Square Houses*. New York: Little, Brown.

Hall, N., et al. 1995. *Looking at Literacy: Using Images of Literacy to Explore the World of Reading and Writing*. London: David Fulton.

Halliday, M.A.K. 1975. *Learning How to Mean*. New York: Elsevier.

Hamilton, V. 1993. "Everything of Value: Moral Realism in the Literature for Children," in *Journal of Youth Services in Libraries*, 6.

Harris, V. 1990. "African American Children's Literature: The First One Hundred Years," in *Journal of Negro Education*, 59(4).

Harris, V. 1991. "Multicultural Curriculum: African American Children's Literature," in *Young Children*, January 1991.

Harvey, S. 1998. *Nonfiction Matters: Reading, Writing, and Research in Grades 3-8*. Portland, ME: Stenhouse.

Heide, A., et al. 1996. *The Teacher's Complete and Easy Guide to the Internet*. Toronto: Trifolium.

Hindley, J. 1996. *In the Company of Children*. Portland, ME: Stenhouse.

Holub, Miroslav. 1983. "Napoleon," in *Gangsters, Ghosts and Dragonflies*, by Brian Patten. London: Piccolo.

Howard, E. 1991. "Authentic Multicultural Literature for Children: An Author's Perspective," in *The Multicolored Mirror*, edited by M. Lindgren. Fort Atkinson: Highsmith Press.

Howard, George S. *Culture Tales: A Narrative Approach to Thinking, Cross-Cultural Psychology, and Psychotherapy*. University of Notre Dame.

Howe, A., et al, eds. 1992. *Common Bonds: Storytelling in the Classroom*. London: Hodder and Stoughton.

Hughes, Langston. 1986. "Aunt Sue's Stories," in *The Dream Keeper*. New York: Knopf.

Hughes, Ted. 1976. "Myth and Education," in *Writers, Critics and Children*, edited by Geoff Fox et al. London: Heinemann.

Hutton, Warwick. 1986. *Moses in the Bullrushes*. New York: Atheneum.

Hyman, Trina Schart. 1986. "Little Red Riding Hood," in *Once upon a Time*. New York, Putnam and Sons.

Iser, Wolfgang. 1974. *The Implied Reader*. Baltimore: Johns Hopkins University Press.

Jeffers, Susan. 1982. *The Snow Queen*. New York: E.P. Dutton.

Jenkins, Carol Brennan. 1999. *The Allure of Authors*. Portsmouth, NH: Heinemann.

Jennings, C. 1991. *Children as Story-tellers: Developing Language Skills in the Classroom*. Melbourne: Oxford University Press Australia.

Johnson, Liz, and Cecily O'Neill. 1984. *Dorothy Heathcote: Collected Writings on Education and Drama*. London: Hutchinson.

Johnson, P. 1997. *Pictures and Words Together: Children Illustrating and Writing Their Own Books*. Portsmouth, NH: Heinemann.

Keene, Ellin Oliver, and Susan Zimmermann. 1997. *Mosaic of Thought*. Portsmouth, NH: Heinemann.

Kellogg, Stephen. 1982. *Johnny Appleseed*. New York: William Morrow & Co.

Kennedy, Richard. 1987. *Collected Stories*. New York: Harper and Row.

Kohl, Herbert. 1995. *Should We Burn Babar?* New York: New York Press.

Kovacs, D., et al. 1991. *Meet the Authors and Illustrators: 60 Creators of Favorite Children's Books Talk about Their Work*. Richmond Hill: Scholastic.

Krueger, Kermit. 1987. *The Golden Swans*. London: Collins.

Kuryliw, Oksana. 1999. "Intertextuality: Stories within Stories," in *Orbit*, Volume 30, Number 3.

Leu, D.J. 1997. *Teaching with the Internet: Lessons from the Classroom*. Norwood: Christopher-Gordon.

Levi, J.H., and M. Rukeyser. 1995. *A Muriel Rukeyser Reader*. New York: Practice.

Lowry, Lois. 1994. *The Giver*. New York: Laurel Leaf.

MacLachlan, Patricia. 1985. *Sarah, Plain and Tall*. New York: Harper and Row.

MacPhee, J. 1997. "'That's Not Fair:' A White Teacher Reports on White First Graders' Responses to Multicultural Literature," in *Language Arts*, January 1997.

Maguire, J. 1985. *Creative Storytelling: Choosing, Inventing and Sharing Tales for Children*. New York: McGraw Hill.

Maguire, J. 1998. *The Power of Personal Storytelling: Spinning Tales to Connect with Others*. New York: Jeremy P. Tarcher/Putnam.

Mallan, K. 1991. *Children as Storytellers*. Portsmouth, NH: Heinemann.

Mann, Peggy. 1973. *My Dad Lives in a Downtown Hotel*. New York, Doubleday.

Marchand, P. 1999. "The Art of the Story," in *The Toronto Star*, November 7, 1999.

Marshall, James. 1972. *George and Martha*. Boston: Houghton Mifflin.

Martin, B. 1967. *The Human Connection: Language and Literature*. Washington: Department of Elementary-Kindergarten-Nursery Education, National Education Association of the United States.

Martin, Bill, Jr. 1987. "A Memoir," in *Children's Literature in the Reading Program*, by Bernice Culinan. Newark, Delaware: IRA.

Martinez, M., & Nash, M. 1995. "Bookalogues: Talking about Children's Literature," in *Language Arts*, 72, November 1995.

Mayne, William. 1987. *Kelpie*. London: Jonathan Cape.

McCabe, Allyssa. 1996. *Chameleon Readers*. New York: McGraw-Hill.

McCall Smith, Alexander. "Children Of Wax," in *Children Of Wax: African Folktales*. Edinburgh: Canongate.

McElroy-Johnson, B. 1993. "Giving Voice to the Voiceless," in *Harvard Educational Review*, Spring.

Meek, Margaret. 1991. *On Being Literate*. London: Bodley Head.

Meek, Margaret. 1996. *Information and Book Learning*. Lockwood: Thimble Press.

Meyer, R. J. 1996. *Stories From the Heart: Teachers and Students Researching Their Literacy Lives*. Mahwah: Lawrence Erlbaum Associates.

Mikolaycak, Charles. 1984. *The Man Who Could Call Down Owls*. New York: Macmillan.

Millard, E. 1997. *Differently Literate: Boys, Girls and the Schooling of Literacy*. London: Falmer Press.

Moline, Steve. 1995. *I See What You Mean*. Portland, ME: Stenhouse/ Markham: Pembroke.

Newland, Alan. 1988. *Language Matters #2 and #3*, edited by Myra Barrs. London: Webber Row Teacher's Centre.

Nicholls, Judith. 1985. "Searcher," from "Moses," in *Magic Mirror*. London: Faber and Faber.

Norton, D. 1985. "Language and Cognitive Development through Multicultural Literature," in *Childhood Education*, November/ December.

O'Neill, Cecily. 1988. "The Wild Things Go to School," in *Drama Contact*, #12, Autumn.

O'Reilly, G., ed. 1999. *The Storymakers: Illustrating Children's Books*. Markham: Pembroke.

Opie, I. and P. 1974. *The Classic Fairy Tales*. London: Oxford University Press.

Opitz, Michael F., and Timothy V. Rasinski. 1998. *Good-Bye Round Robin*. Portsmouth, NH: Heinemann.

Paley, V.G. 1981. *Wally's Stories: Conversations in the Kindergarten*. Cambridge, MA: Harvard University Press.

Paley, V.G. 1998. *The Girl with the Brown Crayon: How Children Use Stories to Shape Their Lives*. Cambridge, MA: Harvard University Press.

Paley, V.G. 1999. *The Kindness of Children*. Cambridge, MA: Harvard University Press.

Paterson, Katherine. 1981. *The Crane Wife*. New York: Morrow.

Paterson, Katherine. 1981. *Gates of Excellence: On Reading and Writing Books for Children*. New York: E.P. Dutton.

Paterson, Katherine. 1989. *The Spying Heart: More Thoughts on Reading and Writing Books for Children*. New York: E.P. Dutton.

Paul, Lissa. 1998. *Reading Otherways*. Lockwood: Thimble Press.

Paul, Lissa. 1999. "Boy Stories, Girl Stories," in *Orbit*, Volume 30, Number 3.

Paulsen, G., and R.W. Paulsen. 1999. *Canoe Days*. San Diego: Harcourt Brace.

Pennac, Daniel. 1999. *Better than Life*. Markham: Pembroke/Portland, ME: Stenhouse.

Philip, Neil. 1991. "The Man in the Boat," in *Scottish Folktales*. London: Penguin.

Reasoner, Charles. 1979. *Bringing Children and Reading Together*. New York: Dell.

Rosen, B. 1988. *And None of It Was Nonsense: The Power of Storytelling in School*. Richmond Hill: Scholastic.

Rosen, B. 1991. *Shapers and Polishers: Teachers as Storytellers*. London: Mary Glasgow.

Rosen, Harold. 1988. "Postcript," in *And None of It Was Nonsense*. London: Scholastic.

Rosen, Michael. 1985. "Shut Your Mouth When You're Eating," in *Quick, Let's Get Out of Here*. Harmondsworth: Puffin.

Rosen, Michael. 1989. *Did I Hear You Write?* Richmond Hill: Scholastic.

Rosen, Michael. 1989. *The Hypnotiser*. London: Andre Deutsch.

Rosenbluth, Vera. 1990. *Keeping Family Stories Alive*. Vancouver: Hartley and Marks.

Rylant, Cynthia. 1982. *When I Was Young in the Mountains*. New York: E.P. Dutton.

Rylant, Cynthia. 1985. *The Relatives Came*. New York: Bradbury Press.

Samson, Florence 1998. "The Personal and Professional Lives of Women Educators." Unpublished doctoral dissertation. Toronto: OISE/UT.

Samson, Florence. 1999. "Teacher Story: Teacher Voice/Student Story: Student Voice," in *Orbit*, Volume 30, Number 3.

Schwartz, Susan, and Maxine Bone. 1995. *Retelling, Relating, Reflecting*. Toronto: Irwin.

Schank, Roger C. 1990. *Tell Me a Story*. New York: Macmillan.

Serraillier, Ian. 1976. "The Visitor," in *I'll Tell You a Tale*. Harmondsworth: Puffin.

Shannon, D. 1998. *No, David!* New York: Blue Sky Press.

Shoemaker, C., et al. 1994. *Write Ideas: A Beginning Writing Text*. Boston: Heinle & Heinle.

Short, K.G., et al. 1996. *Learning Together through Inquiry: From Columbus to Integrated Curriculum*. Portland, ME: Stenhouse.

Short, Kathy Gnagey, and Kathryn Mitchell Pierce, eds. 1998. *Talking about Books*. Portsmouth, NH: Heinemann.

Sims, R. 1983. "What Has Happened to the 'All-White' World of Children's Books?" in *Phi Delta Kappan*, 64 (9), May 1983.

Sinclaire, C., S. Smith and M. Zola. 1995. "Gestures of Space." Unpublished manuscript. University of Mississippi.

Spitz, Ellen Handler. 1999. *Inside Picture Books*. New Haven: Yale University Press.

Steele, Bob. 1998. *Draw Me a Story*. Winnipeg: Peguis.

Steig, William. 1976. *Brave Irene*. New York: Farrar, Straus.

Steig, William. 1998. *Pete's a Pizza*. New York: Harper Collins.

Styles, M., ed. 1989. *Collaboration and Writing*. Milton Keynes: Open University Press.

Styles, M., et al, eds. 1996. *Voices Off: Texts, Contexts and Readers*. London: Cassell.

Swartz, Larry. 1999. "The Best Response to a Story Is Another Story," in *Orbit*, Volume 30, Number 3.

Tejima, Keizaburo. 1987. *Owl Lake*. New York: Putnam.

Travers, P.L. 1975. *About the Sleeping Beauty*. New York: McGraw Hill.

Trelease, Jim. 1982. *The New Read-Aloud Handbook*. New York: Penguin.

Tucker, Nicholas. 1981. *The Child and the Book*. Cambridge: Cambridge Press.

Turner, Ann. 1985. *Dakato Dugout*. London: Macmillan.

Vygotsky, L. 1934, 1986. *Thought and Language*. Cambridge: MIT Press.

Walker-Dalhouse, D. 1992. "Fostering Multi-cultural Awareness: Books for Young Children," in *Reading Horizons*, 33(1).

Walsh, Jill Paton. 1985. *A Parcel of Patterns*. Harmondsworth: Puffin.

Wells, Gordon. 1986. *The Meaning Makers*. Portsmouth, NH: Heinemann.

Wells, Gordon, et al. 1992. *Constructing Knowledge Together: Classrooms as Centers of Inquiry and Literacy*. Portsmouth, NH: Heinemann.

Williams, Linda. 1986. *The Little Old Lady Who Wasn't Afraid of Anything*. New York: Crowell.

Winston, Linda. 1997. *Keepsakes*. Portsmouth, NH: Heinemann.

Witherell, Carol, and Nel Noddings. 1991. *Stories Lives Tell*. New York: Teachers College Press.

Wolf, Dennie Palmer, and Julie Craven, eds. 1996. *More than the Truth*. Portsmouth, NH: Heinemann.

Wolf, Shelby Anne, and Shirley Brice Heath. 1992. *The Braid of Literature*. Cambridge, MA: Harvard University Press.

Wolkstein, Diane. 1978. "I'm Tipingee, She's Tipingee, We're Tipingee, Too," in *The Magic Orange Tree*. New York: Knopf.

Wolkstein, Diane. 1978. "Owl," in *The Magic Orange Tree*. New York: Knopf.

Yolen, Jane. 1972. *The Girl Who Loved the Wind*. New York: Crowell.

Yolen, Jane. 1981. *Touch Magic*. New York: Philomel.

Yolen, Jane. 1986. *Favorite Folktales from around the World*. New York: Pantheon.

Yolen, Jane, and J. Schoenherr. 1992. *Owl Moon*. New York: Philomel.

Young, T., L. Campbell and L. Oda. 1995. "Multicultural Literature For Children and Young Adults: A Rationale and Resources," in *Reading Horizons*, 35(5).

Zipes, J. 1995. *Creative Storytelling: Building Community, Changing Lives*. New York: Routledge.

Publishing Acknowledgments

Every effort has been made to acknowledge all sources of material used in this book. The publishers would be grateful if any errors or omissions were pointed out, so that they may be corrected.

"Our Pond" by Richard Edwards, in *The Word Party* (London: Lutterworth, 1986). "Mouth Open, Story Jump Out," by John Agard, in *Say It Again, Granny!* (London: The Bodley Head, 1986). "Searcher" by Judith Nicholls, in *Magic Mirror* (London: Faber & Faber, 1985). "Shut Your Mouth When You're Eating" by Michael Rosen, in *Quick, Let's Get Out of Here* (Harmondsworth: Puffin, 1985). "The Big Toe" by Richard Chase, in *American Folk Tales and Songs* (New York: Signet Key Books, 1956). "Aunt Sue's Stories" by Langston Hughes, in *The Dream Keeper and Other Poems* (New York: Alfred A. Knopf, 1986). "Napoleon" by Miroslav Holub, in *Gangsters, Ghosts & Dragonflies* by Brian Patten (London: Piccolo, 1983). "Charity Chadder" by Charles Causley, in *Early in the Morning* (London: Viking Kestrel, 1986). *Dear Mr. Henshaw* by Beverly Cleary (New York: Dell, 1982). *I Am the Cheese* by Robert Cormier (New York: Dell, 1977).

We would also like to thank the centre for Language in Primary Education, Inner London Educational Authority, for excerpts from *Language Matters*, #2 and #3, 1988.